DO YOU TAKE THIS WOMAN?

AND MORE DISASTERS

Also by COLIN REID
Life with my Wife: and other Disasters

Do You Take this Woman?

AND MORE DISASTERS

COLIN REID

Drawings by
Colin Reid, Jnr.

CRESSRELLES PUBLISHING COMPANY

FOR THE KIDS

It takes but a second for a bridegroom to answer the question posed in the title of this book—but often a mind-boggling lifetime to understand what it was he agreed to. The episodes here were carved raw from the author's own life, and in one form or another nearly all of them were first chronicled in his weekly column in the *Daily Mail*. They have been collected now as a sequel to *Life With My Wife and other Disasters*. Once again the author wishes to express his gratitude to his wife for promising not to sue him and thanks his eldest son for entering into the spirit of the book and doing the illustrations.

First published in 1973 by
Cressrelles Publishing Company Limited,
Kestrels House, Peppard Common, Henley-on-Thames,
Oxfordshire

ISBN 0 85956 000 7

Printed in Great Britain by Clarke, Doble & Brendon Limited
Plymouth

Contents

8   CONTENTS

1. For Whom the Bell-Bottoms Toll

'HELLO, DARLING, how are you?' she said brightly as I entered the room. 'Had a good day?' She was smiling at me and though she smiles warmly, this one was about 15 degrees warmer on the domestic thermal scale. Something was up.

'I'm fine. Fine, thanks,' I said warily. As a matter of fact, I'd had a pretty tough day at the office as Chairman of the Bring Back the Suspender Movement, but I wasn't proposing to go into that now.

She rose from her armchair with a merry flash of nyloned leg and kissed me. *Something was definitely up.*

Good God, I thought, it's the car! She's hit the garage doorpost again. Not that I'm criticising, mind you. We can't all be hawkeyed judges of garage distance to within a yard or two. But if it was going to be bad news, let's get it over with . . .

As she drew back from the kiss, which had also zoomed up the thermal scale, I was aware that she was still holding my hand. She looked down at it with a little sigh and caressed my palm. 'What nice hands you have,' she said, as though the thought had just occurred to her. 'Hasn't daddy got nice hands?' Any moment now, I thought, the celestial choir and muted violins . . .

'Yes, he has,' chorused the kids, looking at me intently.

Great balls of fire, it's not just the garage doorpost, the whole car's a write-off! It had to be. It was the only calamity I could think of to match the output of loving warmth all round. I could stand the suspense no longer. 'All right, where's the car?' I said. 'What's happened?'

She drew back, frowning. 'What do you mean, where's the car? In the garage, where else?'

'Okay, okay, I've had the good news,' I said, wiping the lipstick off and looking at my lovely hands, 'now where's the bad?'

'Don't be so cynical.'

'Mummy's got a surprise for you!' interrupted the eight-year-old gleefully. I *knew* that, but how much was it going to cost me?

'Don't you dare tell him,' my wife said sternly and walked out of the room, leaving my mind a-boggle. If it wasn't the car what calamity could it be? The house was still standing. There was no smell of burning. The family was present. The cat, rabbit and guinea pig, I could see, were out in the garden gambolling in the sun. There were no new bills around that I could see.

'Right,' I said to the kids, 'let's have it. What is it?'

'No, wait and see!' my 12-year-old daughter giggled. 'We're not to tell. It's a surprise.'

'Is it good or bad?' I persisted. 'I mean, am I going to like it, or what?' A small cloud crossed her face. She appraised me doubtfully. 'I'm not sure,' she said. 'Actually, I don't think so, but . . .'

'Of course sexy daddy won't like it,' shouted the eight-year-old again and began to roll about the floor with mirth. 'Sexy daddy won't like it at all!'

There are times when I worry about that boy. It's always 'sexy' this and 'sexy' that. He watches too much 'sexy' television. But this time he'd got me nailed right. At that moment my wife re-entered the room and the big secret was out. She walked in wearing . . . *wearing what*, for heaven's sake? Bell-bottom pyjamas? A bedroom tent? Something new for summer sleeping? It seemed to be made of a light summery material, gaily patterned, with a clinging top and then belled out to flapping bell-bottoms about fifty inches wide. It was, I decided, something new for horizontal wear on hot summer nights.

She saw the changing, puzzled expressions on my face and said, tentatively, 'It's a trouser suit.'

'A trouser suit?' I said.

A TROUSER SUIT! Did she mean . . . did she mean she was actually going to walk about in it? Around the house? In the *streets*?

The bombshell was bursting slowly, but it was bursting. My wife, my own dear wife, for whom I've worked my fingers to the knuckle and the knuckle to the elbow, standing there before me in a . . . in a pair of street pyjamas! A TROUSER SUIT! And me, the legman's legman, President of the Anti-Trouser League and Chairman of the Bring Back the Suspender Movement. How could she do this to me? How could I hold my head up in the office again?

Clearly, I was nursing a viper in my bosom. Had I not, that very day, been slaving over a hot typewriter producing an article for my girl-mad newspaper in defence of knees? Women's knees, that is. Plump ones, slim ones, smooth, dimpled, naked, nyloned, crossed and uncrossed, but most important of all—exposed knees. That is to say, women's knees which are exposed to the roving and naked male eye, and totally uncluttered by ghastly trousers.

I am aware that already there may be those among you who are muttering, 'Hang about, what's that he said—exposed women's knees? Bit of a dodgy wicket, isn't it? Where could he go from there? What can he write about *knees*, for heaven's sake?' For a knee man—no trouble. Other men choose to be connoisseurs of other areas of women's anatomy. There's the bust brigade, the calf clan, the ankle spotters and the hipsters. According to their fancy, these are the first things they notice about women. Me, I'm a knee man. A quick 1,000 words on the front of women's knees? Just say the word. Another 1,000 on the backs of women's knees? I'm your man. But with trousers spreading, like a blight across the land, where are we knee correspondents? Glum and out of business.

Only this very day I had gone on at considerable length about the unspeakable boredom of rush-hour train and bus journeys where row upon dreary row of typists, secretaries and shop girls were sitting in trousers. What, I had demanded of my readers, was to become of the transcending pleasures of the Knee Game in all public places where knees move and have their being? Where the roving eye could pan the serried ranks of demure knees, shy knees, brazen knees and the lace-exposers where fingertips tug the wayward hem. What was to become of all this?

Apart from the dismal scene for the traveller, what on earth would the great cover-up do to romantic novelists? 'His hand caressed her tweeded knee . . .' No, it just isn't the same.

And now, I had come home to this—a trouser suit by my own fireside. Would not the straight car write-off have been less shattering . . . ?

She stood there before me, a guilty, nervous smile playing at her lips. I stared at the monstrosity. There wasn't a fraction of feminine leg in sight. Not even a toe. Silence hung heavily in the air. She was watching me closely. *Everybody* was watching me very closely, waiting for the judgment.

'I thought,' she said, then hesitated. 'I'd wear it to the party tonight.'

'Party?' My mind had gone numb. I couldn't think of any party. 'Fancy dress party?'

'No, you fool,' she said, a bit irritated. 'Syd's party. It's tonight.'

'Oh . . . oh yes, that's right.'

'But if you don't like it, of course . . .' Tragedy was breaking the back of every syllable as she said it. 'I'll take it back.'

If I don't like it! Me! How could she? Me, who would see every trouser suit manufacturer in the salt mines of wildest Mongolia, just for openers . . .

'Why, uh,' I murmured, clearing my throat, 'it's lovely. Charming.'

Some President. Some legman.

'Oh, do you really think so?' Her face brightened like the morning sun.

'Mm, **y**es, uh, delightful.'

Fleeing from the world outside, what do I find?

What grovelling cowardice is this? Was I, no doubt you are demanding, a mere armchair banner-waver, a critic who would take on the world but wilt before the covered knees of his own wife? How could I, your accusations go on, ever again hold up my head in the Bring Back the Suspender Movement, whose members meet nightly in the saloon bar of my local group therapy centre?

Yes, you are right to raise such serious charges. But hear me out from the dock. I plead temporary insanity brought on by shock. Yes, your worships, shock. There is no other possible explanation. To have fled, I plead, from the trouser suit infested world outside and found, as I fell through the front door with relief, bell-bottoms in my own home . . . your honours, imagine the reactions of a man afraid of ghosts who dashes upstairs to the safety of his bedroom, buries himself far under the bedclothes, shaking with fear, only to feel a cold, clammy hand on his leg under the blankets and hear a deep-throated, sinister chuckle . . . it was more than flesh and blood could stand.

'You really like it then?'

'Mm, yes, very nice,' I intoned in a trance.

'There! I told you he wouldn't like it!' chimed in the eight-year-old sex-pot triumphantly. 'Look at him!'

I was still in a daze when we reached the party, but at least recovered sufficiently to walk ten paces behind her. Who knows, a friend in the League of Legmen could be watching? But how was I to correct this terrible blunder? Clearly, a man cannot go through life walking ten paces behind his wife on her trouser suit days. Something had to be done.

It was then that Fate, as they say, took a hand—or rather a foot. As we walked up the garden path her high heel caught in the swinging left leg of her fifty-inch bell-bottoms and over she went, zonk! onto the edge of the flower bed.

I hastened forward from my rearguard position and helped her to her feet. 'Oh dear,' she said, brushing off the soil. 'I've got an awful feeling it's going to be one of those outfits that something always happens to.'

It was too. Before the night was out it was attacked by a dripping cheese dip and a wobbling red wine glass. 'Just look at that,' she said, baring the stains for my solicitous inspection. 'First time on! What did I tell you?'

'What a pity,' I said, mentally lighting ten candles for the patron saint of the Anti-Trouser League. My mind had now returned to sanity. 'Never mind,' I comforted, 'you could always save it for fancy dress balls. I mean, if you want to go as a Chinese mandarin, or something.'

She glared at me. But I haven't seen the trouser suit since.

2. When the Nibbling Had to Stop

'AND HOW's the Chief Fairy?' said the barmaid cheerfully as she served me a pint in my local group therapy centre. It was a week after the party and the bell-bottom bungle. A sort of sanity had returned to the homestead—though not total sanity.

I took a thoughtful sip at my pint. 'The Chief Fairy,' I said, 'is suffering a bit.'

I should explain at once, of course, that by the term 'Chief Fairy' neither I nor the barmaid meant me. At 14 stone and a devoted legman I don't quite qualify, though I have been known to trip a light fantastic, elf-like, up the stairs in the wee small hours, clutching my shoes and shushing sherbert fumes at the cat. But *c'est la marriage guerre*.

No, the barmaid was referring to my wife, who won the title in a family escapade some years earlier and it's sort of stuck ever since. It had to do with that business of slipping sixpences under the five-year-old's pillow at night in exchange for newly-tugged milk teeth. At least, sixpence was the going fairy rate in most balanced households, but one horrendous night, chronicled elsewhere,* Madame upped the price to two bob. With this cavalier disregard for inflation she not only made a bold bid for Chief Fairy she was the cause of a scene, at five in the morning, in which the five-year-old was discovered in the bathroom trying to tear out all his wobbly teeth. And at such a rate who could blame him? The Chief Fairy had to do some smart back-pedalling on her rates.

'Suffering, you say?' the barmaid said pensively after a moment. 'Well, look who she's married to! Been blotting your

* *Life With My Wife and Other Disasters* (Souvenir Press)

copybook, eh? Rolling home late to congealed dinners again, have you?'

I sank the pint. 'It has nothing, absolutely nothing,' I said firmly, 'to do with me.'

'Oh aye.'

'I haven't rolled home to a congealed dinner in weeks.'

'Oh aye.'

But that there was something wrong with the meal schedule in the house I was well prepared to admit. 'The fact is,' I said, 'the Chief Fairy feels a bit of a fat fairy. She's gone on a diet.'

'Oh, I see.'

I doubt it, I thought. I doubt it very much. When my wife goes on a diet the whole household feels the reverberations. Like earth tremors, they fan out from the volcanic centre as the suffering increases and they shake the lives of every living thing in the house. Even the cat flees to quiet corners under the bed, covering its ears with its paws to cut out the sound of groaning. And I, being too big to get under the bed, flee to the bar, where I stood now, a refugee from a calorie counter.

Looking back on it all, events had followed the familiar pattern. Three mornings earlier I had been awakened by a sort of strangled cry from the bathroom. From deep in the arms of Morpheus I shot up on my elbows, my skin sprayed with goosepimples. What disaster had struck? Had a burglar broken in and attacked someone? Glancing about me for a weapon with which I might belay the villain, I became aware that Madame was not in bed with me and the goosepimples crept higher up my neck. Was she the victim, and even now stretched out on the bathmat?

As I leapt from the bed I became aware that other ears had heard the commotion. Small bare feet were pounding urgently down the landing to the bathroom. 'What's wrong? What's happened?' I heard the urgent inquiries from pyjama-clad figures and at once an instinct which only comes with marriage told me to get back into bed again. Madame was indeed the victim—but only of a pair of brutal bathroom scales. 'I'm up six pounds!' she groaned.

'Oh lord, is that all!' I heard the youngest complain. 'I thought something had happened.' He certainly didn't class *that* as a happening and he, too, went back to bed.

Not that the verdict of the scales should have come as any great surprise to the victim. A couple of days after the party and her bell bottoms went back into the wardrobe she put on a dress, then came to me and said, 'Zip me up, please, darling.' And she wouldn't zip.

'Pull!' she said. There was just a trace of panic in her voice. 'You've done it often enough before.'

True, but it certainly seemed stiffer this time. It must have been all that cheese dip and red wine.

'Go on, pull!' she darned near shouted at me.

So I pulled, almost sprained my thumb, and the zip dived into a plump portion of back. The cat squealed away in terror.

Divorces, of course, have been granted for less, and after she'd given fairly full and vivid expression to her views on the matter, up went the calorie chart on the kitchen wall and it was back to realism and rabbit food.

I may say that the ridiculous thing is she doesn't need to diet at all. The shape is fine, just fine, but try telling her. Like thousands of other women she has to follow the current fad in figures, in which the beanpoles seem to be winning. I keep telling her that a man likes a woman well rounded and that Mae West was right when she said a curve is the most interesting distance between two points. But all she says is, 'What do you take me for? A woman or a road map?'

Anyway, the third day of her Spartan diet she rose with a groan from the TV set and its night-long, calorie-laden commercials. 'Oh God, I can't stand it,' she said. 'Look at them. Every night it's the same, drooling over cakes, steaks, sausages, steaming fish fingers . . .'

'Eggs, fried, scrambled and boiled with soldiers on the side,' I chipped in helpfully.

'Oh . . . and just look at *that*!' she drooled and fled.

That, which finally drove her out to the kitchen, was a big close-up of devilled kidneys sizzling in their succulent juices, with mushrooms, tomatoes and crisp golden chips—in full colour. About 2,000 mouth-watering calories worth, I should guess.

There's no doubt about it, ever since TV gave up cigarettes it has been absolutely stuffing itself with food. It has all the classic withdrawal symptoms of the reformed smoker, and if the IBA has saved our lungs it may yet have to answer for our waistlines.

In the kitchen I knew that the family fugitive from the natural break was steeling herself against temptation, probably doing some rapid stretching exercises. After a moment she came back. 'Would you like a coffee?' she said weakly. She was just in time to catch the last commercial, a large, fluffy sponge cake.

She stared at it hypnotised. For somebody who'd spent three days on lettuce leaves it was too much. 'Or would you like something to eat?' she intoned in a faraway voice.

And here we come to the crunch. When I say that my wife's dieting affects every member of the household, that's exactly what I mean. When *she* goes on a diet *I* get fat. Explain that.

Sure I'll explain that. I used to put it down to an optical illusion. *She* was contracting, I said to myself, therefore I appeared to be expanding. But it wasn't so. I *was* expanding. The evidence was there on the bathroom scales, where one morning I was suddenly struck by a more alarming theory than mere optical illusion. Could it be the same reaction that produced sympathetic pregnancies in men? Because my wife had gone on strike against food, was I, as it were, *coming out in sympathy*?

I promptly went on a diet to counteract my wife's diet and it was then that I discovered the truth. All those tasty dishes she had been yearning for she had been eating by proxy through *me*. She cooked them so she could have a nibble. Well, the nibbling had to stop.

'No thanks, I don't want anything to eat,' I replied as she stood beside me watching the calorie-crammed commercials fade and the TV play start up again (four at a dining table stuffing themselves, of course. What else?)

'Are you sure? I've got some nice——'

'Positive,' I interrupted. 'Just coffee.'

'Oh . . .' It came funereally from her boots. 'I can't tempt you?'

'No, but you have something if you fancy it,' I said.

'No, no, no. I don't want anything. No. No, it was you I was thinking about.'

You bet.

But she didn't weaken. She just produced the coffee, sighed, sat down and with only a slight gulp told the kids not to make so much noise chewing their crisps.

The kids, of course, get it too. 'Eat it all up now,' she says at the dinner table, her eyes diamond-bright on their plates of brimming carbohydrates. 'Is it nice? Good, good. Eat it all up now', she gulps. At these times they watch her like hawks, waiting to rap the darting fingers should they snatch at a chip, which they often do . . . 'Oh, just one! Only one!' 'No, get your thieving hands off!'

But this evening, it seemed she was holding out against temptation. Suffering, but holding out. What I think was still fresh in her memory was her encounter with a store weighing machine earlier in the day. It had all been a bit of a shock. She had stepped onto it hoping it was a kind-hearted one. Such an animal, of course, does not exist. And the verdict of that swinging needle was even more ruthless than on her own bathroom scales, which naturally she tends to muck about with to her own advantage.

There was a sharp intake of breath, a hiss of pure anguish. 'Lord, look at it!' she muttered. 'Will you look at it!'

One thing I'll give her though. When she realises that she's not going to get any mercy out of a public weighing machine there's no one cuter in the ring. It is a rare contest to watch. She approaches it like a boxer moving craftily out of his corner for a championship fight, half-circling, weighing up the sort of attack she thinks it's going to make. After a moment she turns to me as her second and hands me her handbag, her coat, her cardigan and anything else quickly removable that might weigh an ounce or two.

Just as the weighing machine thinks it's got her weighed up she feints with a bit of fancy footwork on the weighing plat-form, whips off her bangles and brooches and hits it with a straight right to the coin slot. Pow! (If it's an 'I Speak Your Weight' type, she's not beyond slapping a hand over its mouth.)

Simple fellow that I am as her second, I think it's all over. But that's only the first round. 'Now you try it,' she says. I'm being used as a calibrator. When the needle whizzes round to something ridiculous she makes some quick calculations about what I weighed on the scales at home, taking into account the fact that my suit was heavier and I had more loose change

Champion dieter K.O.'s weighing machine in
another fixed fight.

in my pocket and promptly announces triumphantly: 'It's reading six pounds overweight!'

Which, of course, is a technical knockout.

Until the next morning, that is, when lying in bed, I hear the day's first roll of tumblers on the bathroom scales and the near scream, 'I've gone UP! How can I be a pound up when I ate *nothing* all day yesterday?' Nothing, mind you, apart from what she nibbled from me and the kids.

Maybe the answer's one of those health farms. I've heard of one not a day's hunger march from the tormented homestead. If I can borrow a wand and wave the Chief Fairy inside for a fortnight maybe I can win us all a bit of peace from the groaning and the nibbling. And I mean all of us—my wife, me, the kids and the suffering cat.

3. All Wives Are Equal, but Some...

THEY DIDN'T BOTHER much with the bride's 'obey' clause in early tribal wedding ceremonies. At the appropriate moment the bridegroom merely boxed his wife's ears and that was that. When the marriage rites were complete he would carry her off to his cave while the assembled guests whooped it up on the applejack—all of them happy in the knowledge of who was wearing the leopard-skin pants.

Later, as the tribes became more sophisticated, the ceremony was adjusted. The bridegroom was presented with a whip so that he could beat his new wife in mime—not only, once again, to emphasise the husband's absolute power but also, a thoughtful gesture, to spare him from bruising his palms.

Since those early splendid wedding ceremonies, marriage has travelled a long way. Whether it has travelled in the right direction is another matter entirely. Today there is a balance of power. The 'obey' clause has vanished and today's brides put rings on their husbands' fingers. Today all wives are equal. Well, that's the idea, but women being the creatures they are, some are more equal than others. Which brings me to my cautionary tale.

This is not to say, by the way, that today's couples do not find much to their mutual satisfaction in their wedded bliss. Of course they do. But it would be idle and foolish to pretend that when one grabs hold of one end of the rope of a modern marriage one doesn't occasionally, even frequently, heave on it tug o' war style, digging the heels in and leaning back on the rope to test the grip at the other end. One does. Not only frequently. It happens all the time.

In these trials of strength one is constantly slithering towards the ditch in the middle, spraying up the mud with threshing heels, gritting the teeth and baying at the moon. A long, long way removed, alas, from the ear-boxing of old. It is, of course, up to each husband to discover in the course of his marriage just how equal his wife is.

Let me, then, set the scene. It was 9.30 p.m. on a Friday evening in late spring and your faithful servant had just rolled into the house with a champagne smile wreathing his happy face. I was, I should mention, two hours late for dinner. I should also mention that it was the third night running.

There will now be a short pause for the quick intake of breath at such wild, foolhardy, cavalier rope-heaving. Three nights in a row? Three dinners dried up and father at the sherbert again? Surely, something had to give? Something did.

But first, please, do not run away with the idea that all I do at nights is knock back champagne and turn up late for dinner. Not true. It merely happened to be one of those weeks known to all men of good intentions and no will power, in which several nights in a row things sort of blow up unplanned, unbidden. Somebody's birthday, somebody leaving the office, somebody arriving, somebody suddenly in urgent need of an ear to bend—and the next thing you know it's two hours past your dinner time and you're smashed again.

And you aren't even *trying* to pull the rope. Right, men?

But if *you* aren't, your wife now is. At least *my* wife now is, or rather was. Wrapping her wrists round what little slack remained, she plonked her high heels into the mud, took the strain and fixed me with a cold eye.

'And what,' she said, the icicles dripping, 'would you like for dinner tonight?'

Now the hidden menace here was that she knew and I knew, *and she knew I knew* that something was already congealing in the oven. Spaghetti and meat balls, actually; now in a dry sauce. So choice didn't really come into it.

But the bubbles, the mad, champagne bubbles had taken over. 'What I rather fancy,' I said, 'is a salmon soufflé. Done rather delicately with asparagus tips in butter. Yes, I think I would rather enjoy that.'

I suppose there are certain moments in history that were set alight by a word or phrase being just right enough, or wrong enough, to ignite the powder keg of revolution. *'Vive la Republique!' 'Let them eat cake,'* etc. Such was this moment.

What put the idea of salmon soufflé into my head I really don't know, but it was enough to divert the kids' attention from TV, which is really saying something. I have never had such a double-take in my life from them.

'A salmon *soufflé*!' gasped the youngest, wide-eyed with awe. Had I leapt from the tallest tree in the neighbourhood, using my umbrella as a parachute, I could not have produced such admiration and wonder.

'With asparagus tips in *butter*!' echoed his sister with an amazed hiss.

'Have you been drinking champagne again, daddy?'

'Have you, dad? Are you sozzled?'

'He's got to be!'

That's when the spluttering fuse hit the powder keg and up went the Chief Fairy. If I may mix my metaphors further— the memory of it all still addles my brain—I tried clinging on to my little bit of rope, but I was yanked smartly and violently across the finishing line into the ditch.

I shan't bother to go into the details of the speech that accompanied this action. Let me say only that she plonked that plate of spaghetti and meat balls down in front of me with such ferocity that even the congealed sauce burst through its outer crust and squirted its juices full in my eye.

As I say, all wives are equal, but some are more so. And ear-boxing days are long over.

4. You, Wife—Me, Pop Star

I HAVE LATELY been contemplating the up and down life of a 'just pop' man. I do not mean Elvis, Tom or Engelbert, who don't sing opera, just pop. I mean me and all the other victims of 'Just pop the kettle on . . .' 'Just pop upstairs . . .' 'Just pop down to the bread shop . . .' and all the other 'just pop' tricks.

'Just pop . . .' is closely related to the 'While you're on your feet . . .' trap and 'Before you sit down . . .' and should always be viewed with extreme caution. Wives, mothers—indeed the whole of the female species—are great users of it.

I've been 'just popping' ever since I was a lad, and my marriage has been popping along for years, with me the pop star. Here a pop, there a pop, everywhere a pop-pop.

The very words 'just pop . . .' are designed, of course, to diminish any task in the eyes, or rather ears, of all right-thinking people, thus making protest impossible, or at the least churlish. This is the first law of 'just pop . . .'

The second law is that the tone of voice accompanying the request is also pitched a semi-octave lower, a low murmur in fact, and delivered in a throw-away, deprecating manner to fool the 'poppee' into further complacency about the task before him. In this way he can finish up doing no end of dreary jobs.

Errands and tasks that started out with a smile and a casual 'Just pop . . .' have involved me in miles of walking, hours of toil and untold expense, of which I, the naïve 'poppee' had no hint.

Only the other day I was jolted to hear the words slipping easily off the lips of one small daughter. 'If you're going out, daddy, would you just pop into the library and get me a couple of books on Paris? We're doing a project.' The library was a mile out of my way and books on Paris in the geographical section were like needles in a haystack.

It is, of course, in the nature of women to wrap up a hard truth in cosy wrapping paper, like 'Just pop . . .' so that you don't notice what's inside until it's too late. 'Just pop down to the church about 1 pm tomorrow, darling, will you? Oh, yes, and bring a ring with you . . .' Well, perhaps not *that* much of a hard truth. But the point is, you don't find men doing it.

Ted Heath is unlikely to ring up his Employment Minister and murmur, 'Just pop into the docks on your way into the office, old man, will you? The chaps are a bit restless.'

Unclear and hopelessly inadequate instructions are invariably part of the 'Just pop . . .' trap. Indeed, to encumber the request with detailed instructions would defeat the object. They would begin to weigh the thing down for what it actually is—a damned big, awkward favour.

The device, of course, has its own built-in hazards. Which is why husbands and sons, told to 'Just pop out for a loaf', come back with every size, shape, colour, texture and make but the right one.

So the wail goes up, *'But all you said was a LOAF! You didn't say anything about a small, cottage-type, hard-crusted oatmeal, unsliced!'*

Of course she didn't. That would have encumbered the thing, complicated it, so that it would become obvious to the 'poppee' at once that he was doing far more than 'just popping'.

Such a request, mind you, is still capable of having bits added to it as you go along, with the prefix phrase, again thrown in casually '. . . *oh, and, while you're at it . . .'* Thus, 'Just pop the kettle on' could mean not only making the tea, getting the cups, saucers and biscuit tin out, too, but if you're not darned careful, preparing mixed grills for ten visiting relatives as well.

However, because of those built-in hazards, the whole popping thing can boomerang disastrously. Which brings me to a note of discord that filtered into the happy home on a recent Saturday morning. As she went out of the front door my wife called out, 'Shan't be long at the shops. Just pop a light under the mince in about half an hour, will you? It's ready on the cooker.'

So that's what I did, popped the gas on under the mince on the cooker and returned to my book. Please note that she said nothing about turning it low, stirring the pot, pouring water on it, or anything else. Just pop a light under it, is what she said and is what I did.

So engrossed was I in my book that I failed to notice the passage of time. But one place it was being recorded was on the cooker. Not wishing to upset sensitive readers, I will skip lightly over the performance she went through when she returned to a smoke-filled kitchen and this burned goo, that had once rejoiced under the name of mince, clinging to her smouldering saucepan. But one thing I've noticed. There's been a sharp drop in the 'just pop . . .' requests. And cheese on toast makes a nice change for lunch.

5. The Happiness Test . . .

MET A CHAP the other day who's just completed his annual dip-stick test on his life. 'Happiness appraisal' he calls it.

'It's not much use being happy if you don't *know* you're happy and the causes of it,' he said over his lunch-time fortifier. 'And most of us live at such a pace these days, rushing from one thing to another, there's no time to assess our lives in total.'

So each year he takes his life, career and relationships out, spends a week giving them a sharp inspection and, if satisfied with the way they're all going, puts them back again. He's on about the summer of his 17th dip-stick, and his latest report to himself, he's happy to say, is: 'No action for another year.'

'What I do is assess a sample week, examine the hours I worked, the reward it paid, re-examine promotion prospects, the time I had for leisure things that interest me, the time I had with my family and face truthfully what gives me the most pleasure. If there's an imbalance in any compartment I correct it. It's a sort of happiness insurance.'

'Maybe he's got something there,' I remarked to the Chief Fairy and assembled mini-minds over breakfast next morning. 'Maybe we ought to try the dip-stick test. I mean, it's no good looking back in years to come—if we're living in the good old days of here and now we should *appreciate* it now. Is everybody happy?'

There was a deafening silence. The clatter of knives and forks stopped like a dawn chorus as the various grey cells homed in on this new target. Even the eight-year-old stopped blowing down his fingers and complaining that his whistle wouldn't wake up.

Unnerved by the silence (what revolution was I starting here?), I went on hastily, 'Let me recap. Happiness is an attitude of mind governed by all compartments in it. Take, for instance, the work compartment in my own week. The humdrum was offset by judging that beauty contest and finding Miss Southern TV. Yes, that was an amusing evening. So I'd probably mark "No change" in the work compartment.'

I was reminiscing pleasantly about the evening when I became aware of Madame eyeing me drily, so I hastened on, 'But everybody to his own bowl of goulash. Happiness for Rousseau, for instance, was a good bank account, a good cook and a good digestion. For Swift it was the perpetual possession of being well deceived. Now how about the rest of us?'

'Can I wish for a good whistle?' frowned the frustrated finger-whistler. It's his latest craze.

'I can fix the whistle for you, son,' I said. 'All you do is bend your tongue like this, see, put your fingers in and blow like thith . . .' I blew. Nothing happened. 'No, like thith . . .' A dull hith, I mean hiss, emerged. I felt the dry look on me again. 'Never mind,' I added quickly, 'I'll show you later. That'll be *your* problem solved for a year. Any more?'

'Less homework and more pocket money would make me happy,' said the whistler's sister. 'Jane gets fifty p, and I only get forty.'

'How about you?' I said to whistler's mother. 'Have you tried the dip-stick test yet?'

'I'd be perfectly happy if you mowed the lawn, which you haven't touched for two months.'

'I don't think you've quite got the idea,' I said.

'Oh yes, I have,' she said.

'No, no. In my own dip-stick test I found I wasn't happy with lawn mowing. Our dip-sticks are getting crossed.'

'But if there's an imbalance in your gardening department it's balanced by that beauty contest you judged and all the girls you were looking at, and I didn't complain about, isn't it?'

As I parted with the increase in pocket money and humped the lawnmower out to the garden, I thought what a damned silly game *that* turned out to be.

6. In Reply to Yours From the Toaster . . .

'WHERE ON EARTH is that letter from the insurance company?' I groaned, flinging around the bills and marbles in the fruit bowl. 'What's *happened* to it?' In some agitation I moved on to her recipe drawer and plunged among the dreams of *coq au vin* and salmon *soufflé*.

She paused with her duster to watch the ritual protest. 'Have you looked,' she said, 'behind the toaster?'

'No, it's not behind the toaster,' I said, a note of edginess creeping in, 'and it's not in the cranny where you keep your handbag and it's not in the magazine rack, and it's not among the guff on the fridge.'

'Well, you certainly won't find it *there*,' she said emphatically, nodding at her invaded treasure chest of recipes. 'Not if it needs answering. What about the bread bin? Have you tried under there?'

I looked. It wasn't there.

'If you put it in that drawer upstairs,' she said, 'maybe it's slipped down at the back again and got mixed up with my underwear. Go and have a look.'

Lord, what a filing system! These are not, as some might think, left-over jokes from National Laughter Week, they are factual observations on the household correspondence file. I defy anyone to match it.

When Mark Twain said, 'Have a place for everything and keep the thing somewhere else, this is not advice, merely custom,' he could never have imagined the system that *my* family would produce—if, indeed, anything of such breathtaking disorder can be called a system.

How it grew I will never know, though probably out of a general disinclination to answer letters, coupled with a fear of letting the kids deal with them. A rough index to it might read as follows:

Letters for immediate action—behind the toaster.

Those whose contents seem confusing and difficult (the majority)—in the cranny where she puts her handbag (there could be a Freudian link here somewhere).

Those demanding money—in the fruit bowl, which also serves as a file for marbles, odd playing cards, pencils and lollipop sticks.

The recipe drawer of pipe-dreams is additionally the dead-end file for souvenirs and letters requiring—or at least will certainly get—no further action.

This 'no further action' also applies, of course, to the recipes themselves. Of the two-and-a-half million that I estimate Madame has cut out and put in that drawer about four have actually reached the table in the form of food.

Not that I'm criticising, mind you. Just facing facts. For as long as I can remember she's been a compulsive hoarder of recipes, snipping them from newspapers, magazines and pamphlets and piling them in the dead-end file with the excited comment: 'Oh, that's a nice one, I must try that.'

But when? Aye, there's the rub.

Yet still she goes on collecting them and still she can say, popping another pipe-dream into her gourmet's guide, 'What on earth shall I do for dinner?'

Once, for the hell of it, I said, 'How about a starter of *sole bonne femme* sprayed with the essence of wild grapes, followed by tournedos rossini in wine sauce, topped with hearts of artichokes and slivers of Cape pears?'

'Away,' she said, lapsing into her native Irish, 'and scratch y'self.'

The trouble is, as she discovered long ago, that she married into a meat and potato family. Put something fancy in front of our lot and they'll glare at it. 'I want bangers!' 'I want fish fingers!' 'What's *this* stuff?'

However, I digress. Back to the filing system, whose final *pièce de résistance* is upstairs in a bedroom drawer. It is a tightly packed, overworked, long-term 'pending' file of assorted communications, from income tax demands to parking summonses, which seems to have an overflow pipe into her underwear drawer. Astonishing, really. I'm sure the whole system is a psychiatrist's Klondyke. It is full of sideshows to distract the attention from the task in hand.

How can you win against a household filing system like this?

Suddenly I'll find myself re-reading and lingering comfortably over old, long-dead correspondence, holiday postcards and the like. These, of course, are the pleasant interludes, but in the despairing ones, as now, when nothing can be found when urgently needed, I wonder whether other people's houses, top people's houses even, operate similar systems . . . 'Mary, what

B

happened to that letter from Roy? It's not behind the toaster. Has it got stuck among your poetry again . . . ?' 'No, dear, have you tried under the bread bin?'

Even perhaps in royal circles? 'I say, darling, what's this new batch of knighthoods doing in my sock drawer . . . ?' No, perhaps not.

One thing I do know, though—the bureaucrats who write to me always seem to want information I can't find. They're mad on numbers—policy numbers, code numbers, tax numbers, National Health numbers. It was an insurance policy number I was after now. And at last it came to light.

'Isn't this it?' she said, putting aside her duster and straightening out a piece of paper. 'It was behind the toaster all the time.'

So it was, but who'd have recognised it? A pair of mini-hands had turned it into a paper dart . . .

7. Girl Meets Gadget

No ONE FALLS in and out of love with a gadget quicker than a woman. No one. Which is why the gadget industry booms and you can't open a kitchen cupboard or drawer without the mind-blowing view of your wife's discarded love affairs.

Toasters, slicers, shakers, beaters, mashers, openers, strainers, grinders, graters, squirters, curved things, round things, wooden things, sharp things, blunt things, funnelled things, things with handles and no batteries and batteries with no handles . . . she's had an infatuation with all of them, each in turn.

Her eyes brightened in the store. A new romance—girl meets gadget. 'Oh look, that's a good idea! I've always wanted one of those.'

'What is it?'

'It takes pips out of pomegranates.'

'WHAT?'

'Yes, they're marvellous. It'll come in wonderfully handy. I'll have one, please.'

Now? Rejected. Forgotten. Lost among the old flirtations. If lucky, one date a year. Oh fickle woman!

To gaze upon such a kitchen collection is to feel like a suspicious husband who flings open the wardrobe door with a cry of triumph and finds the place jammed from rail to rail with elderly, sad-eyed, petrifying milkmen—or even bank managers.

I know. I've just emptied the contents of our alleged cutlery drawer. Among 23 gadgets (excluding knives, forks, spoons, one tent peg, one fuse, two screws, a nail and a bit of sealing wax) five gadgets are still in use—occasionally.

One, a curved, saw-bladed knife for lord knows what purpose, unless to carve bent steak or hunch-backed bacon, never even made it out of the box. It has been lying there under the nut-crackers, apple-corer and egg whisk for at least six months to *my* knowledge. Imagine that! The poor lad didn't even get his coat off.

Oh, Romeo, Romeo what shall we bake today?

And now a new kitchen gadget, the latest Romeo, stands gleaming on the kitchen working surface. A combined liquidiser and food mixer. Madame is in the flush of first love again.

Each morning she enters the kitchen and looks lovingly at it before proceeding with whatever chores demand her attention. And you'd be amazed at the things she can dream up to include her new love. 'Would anyone like some mousse today? Or liquidised meat and potato soup?'

'How about a milk shake?' said the youngest. 'With bananas.'

'Yes, all right,' she said, but a little disappointed that her new love could not be put to a greater test.

How long will the affair last? Clearly the mixer-manufacturer knows the score. He knows his women. With his instruction book came the boldly printed and imploring words, 'Please keep your mixer on your kitchen work bench where you can see it—don't store it away or you might forget it.' I'll say!

It seemed to me that the poor chap was almost on his bended knees pleading not to be jilted.

Mind you, the gadgets that fill a real need and don't merely dazzle with surface attraction will—like real love—always last. Others find new purposes. I have an aunt in the North who always carries her egg-timer to the telephone. She knows her weakness for a good long chat, so she keeps a wary eye on the running sands.

What we could do with, though, are more really *useful* gadgets, like an automatic shirt filleter to remove all those darned pins at the touch of a magnetic button. Oh yes, and there's another one that would come in very handy just now. When I mentioned that I had emptied the contents of the cutlery drawer I forgot to say it was *all over the floor*. All I wanted was a bottle opener, but the drawer stuck . . .

Now why don't they invent something like an automatic wife-soother, some sort of ray gun which you could point at them, and its healing rays would calm them down?

8. The Bank Holiday Picnic

THE FIRST THING to go wrong is the timing.

'Eight thirty on the dot, right? No messing about or flopping around in bed in the morning. Everybody in the car, ready to leave, at 8.30 am. Right?'

Right. You bet. Vigorous nods all round. Stop worrying. It's going to be a great day out. Early start. Miss the Whit Monday traffic jams. Down on the beach by ten. Great.

'Anybody not ready on time gets left behind. Okay?' Okay. 'Even if that includes *everybody*. Right?'

Right, okay, sure, we'll be ready. And for heaven's sake, dad, stop worrying.

So, at 8 30 next morning, where is everybody? In their pyjamas or nighties, or yawning into the bathroom, or playing their flutes in bed, or moaning, 'Lord, look at my eyes!' or 'I knew I should have had my hair done. What a mess!'

Only father is up, dressed, alone and palely loitering in his car, honking the horn in vain. 'Tis but a token protest. He hasn't had his breakfast. The cook is still in the bathroom groaning about her hair. And the morning flute player is yelling that he can't find a clean shirt and how can *anybody* find *anything* in this flipping airing cupboard?

Nine-thirty. Chaos still. Is this a picnic or a troop movement? 'Look, don't bother with the picnic stuff, we'll find somewhere to eat when we get there—*if* we get there!'

'Stop fussing. It won't take a few minutes. And do something useful while you're waiting. Run the vacuum over the living-room for me, there's a good chap.'

Vacuum the carpet! An hour behind schedule already, the

whole of Britain streaming onto the Bank Holiday roads and she wants me to vacuum the carpet! Oh, Drake, you should be living now.

'Who's going to see the carpet, for heaven's sake!'

'Never mind, just do it.'

Okay, so let's leave the place nice and tidy for the burglars again. I hope they appreciate it.

'There now, that's the lot, I think. Chicken sandwiches, hard-boiled eggs, lettuce, fruit cake, coffee, lemonade and . . . what's happened to the crisps? . . . Gavin! Bring those crisps back at once! Now does anybody want to go anywhere before we go?'

Right, yes, that's the ticket, let's get the family bladders synchronised. I'm not searching for bushes every ten minutes because somebody's out of kilter.

'Everybody ready then? Okay, here we go. Ten o'clock. We might make it by twelve—*if* we're lucky.'

'No! Stop! Pull up!'

For heaven's sake! What's wrong?

'Did anybody put the cat out?'

The cat. And me nearly through the windscreen.

Nobody put the cat out. The cat, fleeing from the morning disorder, is still hiding under the flute player's bed, and who'd blame it?

'Oh, can't we take Smokey with us?' No, we can't take Smokey with us. 'Well, I want my boomerang then!'

'All right, all right, *get* your boomerang then! But where you're going to throw it on a crowded beach *I* don't know.'

'Did you put the coats in the boot, dear?' Yes, I put the coats in the boot. *And* the swimming trunks. *And* the towels. *And* the bucket. *And* the spade. We're ready for anything, heatwaves, blizzards, even Australian bushbirds, *and now can we GO?*

'You're sure this jumper goes with these jeans, daddy? They don't clash, do they? You don't think I should change them just before we go, do you?'

'Change them! Who's going to *see* them? It's going to be pitch black by the time we get there!'

'All right, all right, keep your shirt on.'

That's it then, we're off. So everybody settle down. Good. At last. At long last.

'How much farther is there to go, dad?'

Breathe in slowly. 'We've done half a mile, son. Take it off 68 and what's your answer?'

'I'm feeling sick. Dad, I'm car sick again.'

No, don't say it. Just count slowly . . . eight, nine, ten. 'Sit on a newspaper, son, That'll stop your travel sickness.'

'I *am* sitting on a newspaper.'

'Well, look at the scenery then. Look at the lovely scenery out there. It'll take your mind off it.'

'It's boring. Who wants to look at boring scenery? What are you always going on about scenery for? It's boring! And anyway I'm . . . I'm . . . *StopthecarI'mgonnabesick*!'

Oh, God.

'You're not car sick, you're flaming crisp sick! You've been stuffing yourself with them.'

'I think you'd better stop, dear. He looks ghastly.'

'*He* looks ghastly? Look at me! All right, everybody out. We'll picnic here on the Sidcup by-pass.'

9. Fathers' Race

WE STOOD AT the starting line, jackets off, some of us tieless, some shoeless and at least one competitor trying to hide a hole in the toe of his sock. Me.

'When I say "On your marks, get set, go!" ' boomed the man with the megaphone, 'I want you all to run to that bundle of hoops half-way up the track, grab a hoop and bowl it the rest of the way to the finishing line. Right?'

Ahead, on each side of the grass track, bunting-hung under the July sun, the crowd looked back at us expectantly, ready to cheer or fall about according to how the scene struck them. Small children grinned and shouted encouragement. This was the event they had been waiting for. And where else could I be but in the fathers' race? The seemingly comic and good-humoured climax to the day's sports.

And yet, was it my imagination or was there a sharp edge of tension beneath the joking banter as we jostled for position at the starting line? No, it was not my imagination.

'On your marks, get set—GO!' roared the megaphone man, as he said he would, and a split-second later I got a large bony elbow stuck in my solar plexus and somebody's heel on my bare and unprotected toe. Dad had already been nobbled, but this was no time to call for a Stewards' inquiry. I yarooed and dived into the fray.

Gone was the cheerful banter, gone the smiles and jokes and winks. Suddenly wild-eyed men, short ones, long ones, flabby ones, skinny ones, were jabbing, boring and elbowing their way to the front to show their watching families there was life in the old dog yet. And all about us the kids were yelling, 'Come on, dad! Come on, dad! Run!' Their mothers were falling about with glee.

Normally, when this event comes up at school sports days, I go for a lie down, or a drink, or plead a sore finger, so how did I get trapped here? Vanity. Sheer vanity.

When the event was announced the Chief Fairy nudged me from her track-side chair and said, 'Here's your big chance.' Which, as I say, is usually my cue to look at my sore finger or whatever, but before I could do so the nine-year-old groaned, 'Oh no! Don't let daddy go in for it, he'll come in last and embarrass me in front of everybody.'

That did it. That put an entirely different complexion on the scene.

Just because *he'd* come in third in the egg-and-spoon race he did not, I felt, have the right to consign me to my wheel-chair. So I rose, flung aside my coat and made for the starting line, to join a score of other fathers. What is this urge to fight off the years so defiantly?

A couple of ten-yard practice sprints convinced me that I was not only wheezing well but that I might do better with my shoes off—a thought that was striking other fathers, too. Shoes were being dropped at the starting line, but when I removed mine—oh, the shame!—I'd got a large hole in the toe of my sock. I hurriedly covered it with my one good sock, balancing on one leg and glancing shiftily about me. I was trying to look as though I always started fathers' races this way.

There was nothing else for it. Either I ran in my shoes, risked coming last and the withering contempt of a nine-year-old egg-and-spoon champ, or I exposed my naked toe to the world and gave myself an even chance. I plumped for the exposed toe.

What clinched it was the starter's warning that there was only a limited number of hoops at the half-way mark and if you didn't sprint fast enough to grab a hoop you had to leave the race. The shame of having to slink from the track, hoop-less, while the race continued was clearly going to be far greater than the shame of a holey sock. I plumped right.

Elbowing a couple of panting fatties aside and with total disregard for Jockey Club Rules, I seized a hoop and bowled it in behind the leaders.

At the finishing line the No. 3 seed in the egg-and-spoon race beamed. At least I could face *him* again. His mother was another matter.

As I strolled out of the winners' enclosure, her face was a cloud of thunder. 'Get your shoes on!' she hissed. 'Look at the hole in your sock! What are you trying to do—shame me?'

You can't win 'em all.

10. Ten Out of Ten for Strategy

THE IDEA CAME to me the day I found her kneeling beside that part of the household correspondence system that filters down through her underwear drawer. The dead-end file. She was utterly absorbed, reading something.

'How about some tea?' I said.

She looked up, her eyes soft and misty. 'Look what I've just found,' she said. 'It dropped down the back of the drawer.' It was an old school report. Hers.

I read it through, amused. 'Well, well, fancy that,' I said. 'Good at English, I see. Lacks concentration in geography (she hasn't changed—she still has no sense of direction). And excellent at needlework.'

'Yes, I was,' she said, pleased.

Preparing for the Master's report. . . .

'Congratulations,' I said. 'How about some tea?'

She looked back at the report, losing herself in another mist of nostalgia. It was quite sad really, I thought. No more school reports, no more VG for basketball, no more marks in the stinks lab. It was then that I began to warm to my

This housewife must do better next term.

idea: why not have terminal reports on the domestic front?

The constant cry of women, and particularly wives, is that we don't pay them enough attention, that we don't *notice* what they do for us and how they dress for us. And it's certainly true that we all like to know how we're doing in life but get few progress reports.

What I had in mind was little bits of paper that husbands might leave around the kitchen—with six out of ten, say, for washing up, seven out of ten for supper, two out of ten for balancing the budget. That sort of thing. Then perhaps every three months or so we might write a few words in the manner of one's headmaster's report . . .

'This housewife has tried hard this term, but must curb a tendency to spend too much time chatting to the neighbours. General appearance—excellent. Behaviour—mm, er, at times puzzling, shall we say? Must cure her aversion to ironing and will she kindly stop grabbing all the flaming blankets at night? Grade this term . . . B + .'

Of course, she might well entertain herself by doing a terminal report on *him*. That could lead to the odd evening diversion from the telly, which would be something. 'What's this! One out of ten for coming home on time . . . !' Not to mention nothing out of ten for remembering anniversaries.

Here, of course, men are at a disadvantage and must generally rate lower marks. As Arnold Bennett pointed out, 'Being a husband is a wholetime job. That's why so many husbands fail. They cannot devote their entire attention to it.'

However, there are plenty of precedents for end-of-term reports in adult life. Industry uses them, so do the Civil Service and Armed Forces. The standard form in the Navy, I remember, was 'This officer has conducted himself to my entire satisfaction.' Sometimes the signing captain would leave out 'entire', and once I read: 'This officer has conducted himself to *his* entire satisfaction.'

That might be a good one to incorporate in the wife's end-of-term report.

But the whole idea would certainly provide a fresh topic at the ladies' coffee mornings. 'Darlings, I just got nine out of ten for gardening.' 'Marvellous! Congratulations.'

'And guess what! I've just won my Boudoir A levels!'

Yes, we could have some fun with that lot. And such were my thoughts as I turned back to the kneeler at the dead-end file. Perhaps we could discuss it over tea. 'How about the tea?' I suggested.

'Yes, all right, I'll be down in a moment.' she said. 'Just pop the kettle on and put the cups out, will you?'

Just pop, eh? I mentally marked her next report 'ten out of ten for tea-time strategy'.

11. The Wifeless Weekend

'A WEEKEND IN PARIS and no *wives*?' Something close to amazement spread across Charlie's face among the amiable regulars at the bar of my local group therapy centre one Saturday morning. 'You mean that's where you were last weekend? Just you and your two pals?'

'That's it,' I nodded. 'Just me, D'Artagnan and Aramis, my friends in the Escapers' Club.' I was Porthos. Names are suppressed here to protect the innocent. And I mean innocent.

'Cor!' groaned Charlie. 'How did you do it?'

'By train and boat,' I said. 'It made a nice leisurely trip.'

'No, no, you pumpkin. How did you get the idea past your wives?'

'We merely announced it. The women haven't taken over completely yet,' I said, though I had to admit that the idea was greeted with less rapture than the club's little trip to Ireland the previous year, and indeed had to be fed in a drip at a time over several weeks.

Husbands, of course, will be familiar with this slow brainwashing technique. It starts perhaps with a yawn and a totally casual remark during a commercial break. 'Chap in the office was vaguely talking about having a little stag run-out one weekend.' Vague nothing. Every detail's been ironed out.

A week later: 'The chaps are getting quite keen on this idea of a little trip, a sort of break from routine, you know. Might even do Paris.'

For the first time a word penetrates the female grey cells. 'Paris? What do you mean, Paris? What are you talking about?'

'The thing I've been telling you about for *days*. You sat there in that chair while I told you all about it!'

'It's the first *I've* heard of it. Paris? Why Paris? Are you going?'

'Of course I'm going. I told you!'

At the bar Charlie's face broke into a slow grin of relish. 'Gorrr!' he said, picking up his pint. 'A weekend in Paris, eh?'

'It made a nice break from routine,' I said.

'Gorrr! Not 'alf,' he said, nudging me with his free elbow. 'What went on then?'

'Well, we went to the Louvre and had a look round some works of art.'

The grin on Charlie's face erupted into a chuckle. 'Gorrr! Not 'alf,' he said, throwing in a wink.

'On Sunday we visited the Sacre Coeur and Notre Dame and listened to some of the sermons. Very good acoustics.'

The chuckle broke into a guffaw. 'Cor! Weekend in Paris very good for acoustics. Come on now, cut out the double-talk, let's have the facts! Saturday night now, what did you get up to on Saturday night? And none of your acoustics!'

'Saturday night? Ah, yes, that was particularly pleasant . . .'

'Yeah! That's it!' enthused Charlie. 'Spill the beans.'

'Well, the three of us in our Escapers' Club—coming as we do, of course, from the world of newspapers—were invited along to a sort of literary salon where we discussed the Common Market and the French political situation.'

Charlie began to fall about the bar and had to put down his beer for fear of spilling it. 'Look at him! Just look at him!' he chortled. 'Handing it out deadpan! You ought to be on the stage, mate!'

The truth, I have come to learn, is a very difficult commodity to sell.

Charlie leaned weakly against the bar, rubbing his eyes, from which tears of mirth were spilling. 'Are you—are you going to tell us anything, anything at all?' he gasped.

What was the point? I was on a hiding to nothing. I could have told him many things about that delightful weekend in

Paris—that the food is still fabulous, the prices fierce, that the Metro runs on rubber wheels, that I didn't see a mini-skirt the whole weekend, that the French girls no longer match British girls for lively attractiveness, that everywhere women greet each other with kisses and that everyone is still shaking hands like mad. But Charlie was clearly in no mood to believe a blind word I said. The image of 'Paris without wives' was too deeply ingrained for me to remove it.

'Sorry,' I said. 'Got to be off now. I have to cook the kids' lunch.

For the first time Charlie's face began to straighten up. 'What? Has your wife walked out on you then?' he said.

I hesitated about whether I should pass on the next bit of information, then plunged in. 'No, I've been left in charge,' I said. 'She's flown off to Paris for the weekend with two of her friends.'

The grin was returning again. 'And no husbands?'

'And no husbands,' I said.

'You mean a rival club? Tit for tat?' He was falling about the bar again.

'Yes, a rival club,' I agreed. 'All wives are equal now, didn't you know?' And I didn't get it fed a drip at a time.

As I reached the door he called out. "Suppose she tells you,' and he began to roll about the bar again, 'she's been to the Louvre and listening to the acoustics?'

'I shall believe every word of it,' I said. 'And *bonjour* to you.'

12. Uncle Colin's Casebook

IT'S IMPOSSIBLE for a chap to operate on my sort of platform as a sex-war correspondent without being regarded from time to time as some sort of wife-handling whiz-kid, an omniscient oracle of the domestic scene.

Rather touchingly, husbands tend to sidle up to me in bars, glance furtively over their shoulders and mutter, 'You're just the chap. Look, I've got this problem . . .' They then describe the symptoms and expect me to prescribe the remedy. A classic case of the blind leading the blind, of course, as we have already seen, but I do what I can.

Just because I write about women in my column, now and then, it doesn't mean that I understand them, I tell my patients. Indeed, if all women were understood nobody would write about them. It's not like, well, walking, say. Newspapers and magazines are not filled with such advice as 'To walk it is necessary to place one foot in front of the other in alternating succession, leaning slightly forward to gain the necessary momentum.' We know about walking. It is a perfectly natural process which we understand. Women, on the other hand, are not a natural process. To walk is easy. To woman is not.

However, I always listen patiently to those who come to my clinic in the saloon bar of my local group therapy centre.

I listen for three reasons. First, I might learn something. Secondly, there's a therapeutic value in being listened to. Thirdly, my consultant's fee is always paid in free drinks. Though this can have its hazards. After a busy night in the consulting room there have been times when I, too, have needed a consultant, preferably one with an honours degree in wife-handling.

Mostly, I've noticed, my patients seem to go in for mysteries. Consider a typical night. There I was, leaning on my consulting room desk, nursing a fee, when this chap Graham came up to me and asked me if I'd got a remedy for domestic chain reaction.

Ah, domestic chain reaction—yes, I knew it well.

His particular problem had started when he bought a new plug for his cooker. All he wanted to do was fit the new plug, but it required pulling the cooker away from the wall. And he told his wife so (that was his first mistake). His wife saw what a mess the back of the cooker was in and decided they should clean it.

Having cleaned it, she decided they couldn't possibly push it back against that dirty part of the wall where the cooker had blocked it. That needed cleaning, too. Hubby was handed the cloth. Having cleaned *that*, his wife decided it made the rest of the wall look pretty grubby and would he mind helping her wash that down, too? Which kind of threw up the grubbiness of the other three walls . . .

As he was backing into his dining-room on his hands and knees, scrubbing the floor, Graham finally rebelled and called a halt. 'If I hadn't,' he said, 'I'd have been in the hall, up the stairs and probably finished up painting the house. All over one lousy plug.'

A textbook case of domestic chain reaction. What he should have done, of course, was fit the plug in secret and say nothing. 'Never let wives see you manhandling any domestic equipment,' I counselled him. 'They think they've got you *in the mood*. Give 'em an inch and they'll grab a mile of you.'

He looked so glum I hardly liked to take his fee. But I did.

NEXT CASE . . .

This was a puzzled patient called Syd, to whose flower-bed I owed the execution of the Chief Fairy's bell-bottom trousers and I was therefore gratefully prepared to waive my fee.

'I go out and buy three pairs of socks. Right?' said Syd. 'One blue pair, one yellow, one red. Right?'

'Right,' I said. All was crystal clear at the moment.

'So I wear them, chuck them in the laundry basket and my wife puts them in the washing machine. Right?'

'Right.' Complications, I could see, were setting in.

'So why the hell do I only get three odd socks back? One red, one blue, one yellow. Who steals odd socks?'

I pondered. 'Have you,' I said, putting the tips of my fingers together in the best consulting room manner, 'got a one-legged lodger in the house?'

'Of course I haven't got a one-legged bloody lodger in the house,' he said.

I nodded sagely. 'In that case,' I said, 'I cannot help you. You're another victim of the End-Mover——'

'A *what*?' interrupted Syd.

'A mysterious poltergeist that moves around houses hiding all those things you can't lay your hands on. His greatest joy is to hear the cry, "Who the devil's moved my . . ." ' 'It attacks the household finances, too, from which it derives its name. When you're just about to make both ends meet, he's the one who moves the ends. He's probably one-legged, too.'

'Put a sock in it,' said Syd.

NEXT CASE . . .

Ah, yes, poor old Fred. This was a tricky one. Sad-eyed, he bewailed the fact that his wife never asked him to unzip her dress any more. The romance had gone out of his life. She now unzipped herself with some trick she had with a wire coat-hanger, hooking it onto the zip and yanking it up and down behind her back while Fred sat on the bed looking on glumly. No wonder he was in the bar.

Life wasn't the same any more. He felt, well, sort of excluded. A bit spare. Not needed on voyage. For a moment he lapsed into silence, staring into his beer as though it might hold the answer. But it didn't, so he turned back to me. 'How about that?' he asked.

I agreed at once that the words 'Zip me up,' or 'Unzip me, darling,' were part of the weft and weave of a happy marriage and it was a bit thick that a healthy red-blooded fellow could be replaced by a coat-hanger—particularly a free one from the cleaners, which apparently it was. That was rubbing salt in the wound.

But many strange things were happening in the world today, I told him, and it would probably get worse before it got better. He could, of course, go round the house hiding all the coat-hangers, I said.

For a brief moment Fred's eyes lit up at the thought of this counter-ruse, but it wouldn't get to the root of the problem, I added. It wasn't only the march of science, devising coat-hangers to take the fun out of the hands of men, it was the march of New Liberalised Woman. Husbands were going to have to find themselves a new role.

Fred's gloom deepened as he slumped over his beer. What we have to face, Fred, I said, is that the defenceless, helpless, fluttering-eyed female has gone and it won't be long before you're fetching your wife's pipe and slippers.

It was all too much. Fred gave a low moan. Had I no words of encouragement for him? Wasn't there any advice from Uncle Colin's Casebook? Did this woman's liberation mean that the zip was to leave his life for ever?

Not quite, Fred, I said, there was still hope. His shoulders twitched. He raised his head and above his empty glass he caught the barmaid's eye. No, not there, Fred, I said, not there, YOU've got to get back to basics.

Return home now, I said, and choosing your moment, ask your wife if she'd mind just putting down the hanger and assisting you with your braces. And maybe once in a while perhaps she could give you a little wolf whistle. Try it, Fred, I said . . . Fred?

But Fred was lost in the eyes of the barmaid.

13. In the Quick, Quick, Slow Life of a Wife

MOST ALARM CLOCKS—modern production-line jobs with no imagination, no personality—trot dutifully up to the bell at the same monotonous rate and ring. They have no panache, no sense of humour. They roll off their production belts uniformly dull.

But I once had a timepiece with real personality, a clock with gaiety in its soul, an individual. A battered, twin-hatted wonder called Aggie. Not for that one the dreary round of robot punctuality. Aggie liked to approach her bell with a sense of adventure, a hop, skip and a jump, with a quick sprint or two thrown in to vary the pattern.

Sometimes, as she entered the straight to the bell, thumping out her broken tattoo, she would stop altogether for several seconds, then turn on the alarm from apparent death. It was a horological *tour de force*. The hit of her repertoire.

Aggie was old, of course, very old, a junk-shop bargain from a forgotten age, but I was fond of her and would pander to her weaknesses. For instance, her failing bell power I used to mollycoddle in a soup plate on the bedside table. The plate provided a simple echo chamber to magnify the bell and rouse the deepest sleeper. And there was always TIM to dial, if in doubt.

Alas, Aggie is dead and gone. Some said it was a broken spring, but I think it was a broken heart when we retired her in favour of a young, brash, brain-washed factory job. A sad day.

What brought Aggie to mind was an incident the other morning. I was galloping along to the station with about three

Alas, poor Aggie! And we still don't know the time.

minutes to catch a train and fiercely wondering, not for the first time, what it would be like to live in a house where all the clocks tell the right time.

Aggie may have gone in the name of efficiency, but we still haven't a clock in the place that tells the truth, the whole truth and nothing but the truth. It isn't the built-in mechanical errors so much as all the counter-espionage jiggery-pokery that goes on from my wife. Like several other women I know, she seems determined to protect her family from the Correct Time; putting on this clock, letting that one slow down or even stop altogether, according to her plan of action for swindling herself and everybody else through the day's routine.

On this particular morning the bedroom alarm was 15 minutes fast and the kitchen clock five minutes slow. What the running order would be the following morning is anybody's guess.

If she has an early appointment at the hairdresser's the bedroom clock is liable to be an extra ten minutes fast. This way she can still claim her ten-minute extra ziz after the alarm has gone off and comfort herself that it's not so late as it looks.

In the kitchen the strategy is to reverse this piece of double-think. And if you know the darned clock is slow—how *much* is it slow?—it can certainly stop you dawdling over your corn-flakes.

You can see those schoolroom unitary sums going on in the kids' heads as they stagger in for breakfast. Solve the following: 'If the bedroom clock in A's house shows 8.45 and is 25 minutes fast, the living-room clock shows 8.30 and was 10 minutes fast yesterday, but losing at the rate of one minute a day, what is the right time if the kitchen clock is X minutes slow and today's the day for Mrs A. to visit the hairdresser and do the shopping?'

You need more than an 11-plus mind to solve that one and I could see my small daughter struggling with our own version of the problem in the kitchen. Finally, she hazarded: 'Is it half-past eight, mummy?'

'Yes,' replied her mother.

'Oh no it isn't,' I said with a touch of triumph. 'It's only twenty-past. I put the bedroom clock on ten minutes last night to get your mummy out to the theatre. You know what they're like.'

Madame gave me a cool look. 'I know you put it on. That's why I put it back.'

Which is how I came to be galloping along to the station with three minutes to catch a train . . .

Aggie may be dead, but the malady lingers on.

14. The Bride Who Came in from the Cold

THE HAPPY DAY dawned clear and bright, as we hoped it would, and by 8 am the bathroom resembled Piccadilly Circus. Maxi-people and mini-people bustled in and out in various stages of their finery, and the air was filled with 'Do you mind if I do my eyebrows?' 'My hair?' 'My teeth?' 'Can I get a hair-clip?' No, no, not at all. Help yourself.

There's nothing like a family wedding for demolishing bath-room protocol. Once again another bright-eyed, eager young male was preparing to face that all-vital question, 'Do you take this woman . . .?' As an older cousin of the bride, I had gone north for the ceremony to lend support and guidance, drawing upon my own extensive knowledge of what an 'I do' to that question actually entails.

As I stood there now in my see-through vest, mowing the morning bristles in the shaving mirror and pom-pomming the bridal march, I was interrupted in mid-pom-pom by Madame. 'Have you decided,' she said, hogging the mirror to fix her lipstick 'what you're going to say?'

'Say?' I queried. 'About what?'

'Your speech.'

'Ah, yes. Mm. No, I haven't,' I said. 'I've no doubt some-thing will spring out of a bottle at the appropriate moment, once we've got the church bit over and started the festivities. All they want, I suppose, are a few words of encouragement from cousin Colin. Something to speed the happy couple on their way. Why?'

'Just be careful wogooroosaysall . . .' The rest of her remarks were lost in incomprehensible gibberish as she rolled her lipstick on her flexed lips, still talking. She's always doing it.

Patiently, I removed the lipstick from her fingers. 'Run that spool again, will you?' I said.

'Just be careful what you say, that's all. The other side don't know you as well as we do.'

The other side? I paused, shaver in hand, mulling over this new development. *The other side?* What strange remark was this? She made the bridegroom's lot sound like the enemy opposition in a spy thriller. Were Smersh going to be there, too? In the excitement of the morning my mind began to take flight. Was I being used as cannon-fodder in The Bride Who Came In From The Cold? Goosepimples began to creep up the back of my neck.

'I shall watch it very carefully,' I said, measuring my words slowly. 'Very carefully indeed.' And so I did.

In church I watched my cousin M usher the guests to their pews. As he led them down the aisle I noticed that he put our lot on one side and the other side on the other side. Significant. M was taking no chances.

'What do you know of the other side? I whispered to M behind my hymn sheet. It was M's sister who was getting married.

'They're very nice people, you'll like them,' he whispered back, *glancing over his shoulder at the other side*. Was M a double agent? 'They're from Scotland,' he said. So! They'd infiltrated over the border to deepest Cheshire for this match. I narrowed my eyes at them over hymn 632.

The ceremony, however, passed without incident, apart, that is, from much gulping back of tears as the bride, from our side, stood with the bridegroom, from their side, and the hymn-singers soared into *O Perfect Love*. There was a fair stretching of emotions on my own immediate side, too, I can tell you. She almost had me at it.

'That was the hymn we had,' she said, all dewey-eyed and pulling out her handkerchief. So it was, but I recalled it very nearly wasn't. The hymn I actually asked for was *For Those in Peril on the Sea.* I asked for it in all innocence because I happened to like it, and was unfamiliar with wedding protocol. But the vicar said he didn't think it was appropriate. I don't know though . . . and anyway it wasn't as though I'd asked for *Fight the Good Fight.*

As the young couple emerged from the church into the sunshine the confetti and the handkerchiefs fluttered, and that was the image uppermost in my mind as I was called on to address a few words to the assembled company at the wedding reception.

It had been a wonderfully happy day, I said, casting a quick glance at the other side, and therefore was it not mystifying to see all the women crying?

'There are those,' I went on, 'who say that women cry at a wedding because they know what's going to happen, and the men are happy because it isn't happening to them.' Was it my imagination again or did I detect a stiffening in the faces of the Smersh lot? I felt the goosepimples rise again, so I quickly leapt onto safer ground. 'Ah, but I am not among them,' I hastened on. 'I am not among them at all. I am a great believer in marriage. I even have a wife to prove it.'

The threatening faces relaxed. Smersh smiled. I was safe from attack. At least I was safe from Smersh. That was all. I should have known. In any good spy story the surprise attack comes from your own side, and it came from mine. 'Ow!' I yelped as I felt a sharp tap on the shin under the table. It was Madame. 'I told you to watch it,' she hissed.

Smersh not only smiled, they laughed outright. They'd got an agent on the other side.

15. Let's Get Out of this Joint

THE WARY YOUNG BRIDEGROOM stepping onto the skating pond of marriage is well advised (as I counselled my newly-married cousin) to look out for the danger notices marking the thin ice.

These are not, as he might think, the ones that bear the words 'his' and 'hers', or even 'yours' and 'mine'. Beneath such signs the ice is solid and he may stamp across it with confidence. *His* toothbrush, *her* towel, *his* books, *her* wardrobe, *his* fault, *her* decision—there is no danger here. No, the sign to beware of is the one that says, or rather shrieks, '*Ours*'.

Here the cracks in the ice fan out ominously over the chilly waters of shared things, the joint account, the joint toothpaste (*sans* cap), the joint anniversary. Perhaps you've heard of someone's marriage aching at the joints. This is what they mean.

Take the joint account, which, according to its state of health, can be either *his* overdraft or *our* money. The monthly examination of the bank statement is usually accompanied by much prodding at old cheques and anguished cries of 'What's *this*?' 'When did you buy *that*!' 'Never mind that, look at all these cheques signed to the club! What have you been doing up there?' And so on as the happy skaters sink slowly through the hole in the ice.

Each couple have their own danger areas marked out, of course, but the thinnest ice on my own pond bears the warning, 'Our car'. At least it's our car when it doesn't need washing or repairing, then it becomes his car. Or rather mine.

But the real danger area here developed the day she passed her driving test. Now I know that the Ministry of Transport say she can drive. They gave her a licence as a mark of their confidence. The question is: 'Shall I let her drive with me in it?' I mean it's all right for the Ministry of Transport. They're not actually sitting there beside her, are they?

My problem is that once in a moment of short-sighted folly I did what no husband should ever do with his wife: I gave her her first driving lesson. One lesson, that's all . . . it was enough. All right, so I'm a coward. But each man is the sum and victim of his own experience, and he should not be mocked if life has tended to litter his path with banana skins. That experience lives with me still and has long been an area of dangerous sensitivity between us.

In the beginning, when she first discarded her 'L' plates, I avoided the open confrontation of who was going to drive whom by getting to the car first, in a casual sort of way. 'Just getting the car out of the garage,' I'd call cheerfully, sprinting out of the front door. And that would be *me* behind the wheel, and her in the passenger seat.

The pattern became established and for the sake of our nerves she tacitly accepted it. But lately there have been signs of simmering rebellion. When she has driven to the local station to pick me up at night her eyes are watching me. Which side of the car will I climb into? The driver's or the passenger's? She keeps waiting for the vote of confidence, and the other evening I gave it to her.

It had not escaped my notice that for a long time now she and the car had been arriving at the station in one piece. So I got in on the passenger's side.

She looked at me amazed. 'Do you want me to drive?'

'Sure. Go ahead,' I said, and no sooner had I said it than I could feel the hairs standing out on the back of my neck. What had come over me? What mad folly was this? But it was too late to back out now.

To try to demonstrate my confidence I rested my hand against the dashboard in what I hoped was a relaxed sort of way. My arm was as rigid as iron. Casually I stretched out a foot in front of me, but beneath it I was applying such pressure to an imaginary brake that it was in danger of going through the floor.

I remember nothing of the journey other than the fact that we set off in one piece and arrived in one piece. But she could have driven like a Brands Hatch champion and it wouldn't have made the slightest difference. That earlier experience with the 'L' plates was all too deeply ingrained to eradicate.

'How was I?' she asked, a small note of triumph in her voice, when we pulled up outside the house.

'Fine, fine,' I said, removing my foot from the phantom brake and my rigid arm from the dashboard.

The mistake I made was closing my eyes and breathing out in pure relief. I thought she was looking the other way but she saw it all. 'God, how can anybody drive with *you* sitting there like *that*!' she exploded and in no time at all there we were, sinking through the hole in the ice.

16. Bottoms Up

WHICH END of a boiled egg do you put in an egg cup? Sharp end? Flat end? You don't know? You don't care? And what do I think I'm doing tiring out your eyeballs with such trivia?

Yes, I'm well aware that some of you are already shaking your heads and tutting, 'Tsk-tsk, hasn't this fellow anything more important to concern himself with? Which end up does a boiled egg go, indeed!' The flat end of course. Any fool knows that. On with the next business.

And true, at first glance, the matter hardly seems to rank among the great dilemmas of our time. Among such questions as 'Should we stay in the Common Market?' 'Bring back hanging?' 'Ban pornography?' and 'Cut the beer tax?' the dilemma 'Which way for a boiled egg?' hardly seems to count as a front-runner. But that's only at first glance.

Come with me into the deeper recesses of this egg problem and I shall show you which way the world is going, what future awaits Man—anarchy, stability, intolerance, patience, materialism, ideals and ethics. It's all there to be read in our egg cups.

But first a declaration of interest. I'm a sharp end man myself. I always put a boiled egg in an egg cup sharp end up, blunt end down. Always have. Always will. And so far as I know, only one person refuses to accept this. My wife.

In all the years we have been married, while seeing eye to eye on many matters of mutual interest and pleasure and having reached successful compromises where we differed, this is one area in which there has been total and apparently irreconcilable deadlock. You really wouldn't believe it.

Shattering rows have flared, and still flare, over it. To this day, *to this very morning*, she still insists on putting my egg in the egg cup upside down. She says it's the only way to eat a boiled egg—flat end up. And every single time, year in, year out, I have to turn it over, flat end down, before assaulting it with my spoon.

Breakfast, and another flat-end rebel defends his boiled egg.

She can *see* that I turn it over. I *tell* her that I'm turning it over. I do it with much noise. I point out that the yolk is in the base of the egg and that penetrating the shell from this end will result in the egg spilling its golden juices down the side and that I shall be left with only the hard white.

But it makes no difference. I still get the egg upside down. And either we have another argument about it, or she pretends not to notice, like ignoring a terrible skeleton in the family cupboard . . . 'Sssh, everybody! Colin eats his egg with the bottom up.'

This is bad enough, but there is worse. She is bringing up my children to be flat-enders.

Whenever boiled eggs are served for breakfast, I always make a point of reversing everybody's as well as my own. It may strike a visitor as an odd way to conduct a breakfast, but that's the way it has always been. As the Chief Fairy pops the eggs into the egg cups, I go round the table up-ending them.

Until recently I had met little resistance from the rest of

c

the family, but the other day there were loud protests from one small son. 'Stop turning my egg upside down!' he protested hotly. I went pale.

'But that's the *right* way up,' I said. 'The other way all the yolk will be at the top.'

'I *want* the yolk at the top!' he shouted, working himself into a bit of a lather. 'I don't want to have to go through all that white stuff to get to the yolk!'

I went paler. You can see where all this is leading, can't you? There's more to this than a boiled egg. We have all been well enough taught by the experts in behaviour, body language, touch and other outward signs that reveal the innerness of people to know *that*, though perhaps I am the first to reveal the secrets of the boiled egg.

Clearly, you don't need to be an egghead to see that the man who puts his egg into an egg cup blunt end down is a no-nonsense type who likes to see a solid base to life. He's prepared to work hard (spooning through the egg white) for his rewards (the yolk) and applies himself with patience and discipline to the task.

His opposite, on the other hand, has no patience with such approaches. He wants his yolk *now* and he doesn't care how he gets it, even if it means standing the world (the egg) on its nose and in the process letting some of life's treasures spill wantonly away (yolk down side of shell).

See? This is what Hollywood meant when it used to say: 'This thing is bigger than both of us.' It's not just you and a boiled egg. It's the whole future of the world at stake.

But how can the world bring up its children to the right values if people like my wife keep egging them on (sorry about that) to be flat-enders?

17. The Morning After

He came thundering up the stairs, rattling his tin of marbles in a mind-splitting din. 'What's a hangover, daddy?'

'Please go away,' I explained. 'Please.'

I shrank my head into my shoulders and gritted my eyes shut. In some odd way it helped to reduce the noise.

'What are you crawling on your hands and knees for, daddy? Is it a game? Can I play, daddy?'

'No.'

'Shall I ride on your back?'

'NO!' Oh God, my nerve ends again.

'Are you looking for something?'

'No, and please stop shaking that tin of marbles!'

The horizontal hold on my eyeballs kept slipping and I was getting sound on vision. The palsied hands groped forward and I felt his interested eyes watching my progress along the landing carpet to the bathroom.

'Mummy, why is daddy crawling on his hands and knees like that?'

'Perhaps,' she said, calmly removing sheets from the airing cupboard and taking absolutely no notice of her mate at death's door beside her feet, 'he feels safer down there this morning, dear.'

He watched me crawl into the bathroom. 'What's he putting his head on the tiles for?'

'He just feels like it, I suppose. Daddy met some old friends last night and forgot his way home.'

'*Aaaaaaaaaah!*'

'What did you say, darling?'

'Look! Daddy's put his head under the tap. Is he washing his hair?'

'*Aaaaaaaaah!*'

'What's that, darling? I can't hear what you're saying.'

'Take that tin of marbles off him! My mind's disintegrating!'

'Go out and play with your marbles, dear, there's a good boy. Leave daddy alone. He had too much wine last night. He's got a hangover, as I told you, that's all.'

That's ALL! May Bacchus forgive you! How can you mislead the lad? Tell him the truth, the facts of horror of the morning after. One day he, too, may face the temptations of the grape and the grain. He, too, will bump into old friends and go to parties and know the laughing, bubbling madness of a New Year's Eve. Tell him, *please*, about January the First as well. Tell him of the time bomb at the bottom of the bottle. Tell him of the awakening when the happy anaesthetic has worn off and the head thumps and the hand shakes and the eyeballs throb in their sockets.

Tell him of the morning mysteries. Who came in the middle of the night and re-lined his throat with sandpaper and replaced his tongue with the insole of a Desert Army boot? How can voices from so far away deafen him and who re-wired his central nervous system to a slimming vibrator? How could the gay, witty, singing chap of the night before be reduced in a few hours to this quaking, seedy, palsied being?

Why do his children pick this morning of all mornings to jump on his bed and bounce up and down and blow whistles and flutes and shake marble tins and wind up the noisiest toys they can find? Who tipped them off?

Why, knowing it all, will he vow never to touch another drop as long as he lives and still be there the next time, slapping his thigh at the bar and chuckling, 'All right then, just one more?'

And, finally, why in this day and age when men can reach the moon and play musical chairs with human organs, can't someone invent a *real* hangover cure?

Such questions raged through my mind as I hung my head under the cold water tap and let its icy juices spray the throbbing. Nor was it the only chill about the place. I knew there was more to come. But let us return briefly to the night before the morning after . . .

Having got side-tracked at an impromptu celebration on my way home, I arrived late but full of bonhomie. 'What ho!' I said or some such pleasantry. She was about to depart to bed.

'Where the devil have you been?' she demanded.

I'm fairly quick off the mark in this sort of situation and I could tell all was not well. The frost was already crackling in the air and the mercury plummeting Arcticwards.

'Why? What's up?' I fenced cagily.

'*Why?* Because I've been sitting here for three hours and I've just sent the baby-sitter home! *You said you were taking me out to a party tonight!*'

Oh boy. She was right. By golly. 'I'm sorry—I—er, forgot,' I groaned, which was the astounding truth, but of little solace to her.'

'You forgot!' and that's when the marital mercury fell out of the bottom of the thermometer. And if, the next morning, I found her more concerned in removing sheets from the airing cupboard than with my moaning figure on all fours, I suppose I have no one to blame but myself.

And so to breakfast, among the icicles . . .

'I wonder whether,' she said, looking up after some time reading the morning paper, 'I could swop you.'

Swop me! I knew where she'd got the idea from. She'd been riveted by a tale in the paper of marriage-swopping and now looked at me pensively.

My head was clearing rapidly. Perhaps this was the hang-over cure I needed. I thought for a moment, then said guardedly, 'For keeps? Or just for lends?'

The marbles player, recognising the language, paused at his breakfast-munching. 'Are you going to get a divorce?' he said interestedly. There followed one of those Pinteresque silences broken finally by the marbles player. 'Is it because daddy's been turning the boiled eggs upside down again?'

'No,' I said, and thought I caught a brief flicker of a smile on his mother's face. 'Not a divorce. Your mummy's thinking more in terms of a trade-in for another model.'

No sooner had I said it than I suddenly had a nightmare vision of the shape of marriage to come: A Used Husband Mart, probably with its own magazine like the second-hand car market, offering trade-in bargains . . .

So Madame would like to trade in her old man?

'1952 husband, one owner, well run in, near-immac. cond. Immediate delivery. Owner seeks change to Sagittarian, cash or near offer.'

Or '1946 vintage model, well oiled, fair wrkg order. Exterior needs attention. M.O.M. (Ministry of Marriages) tested. Suit Fleet owner. Exchange for '62–'64 sporty model, sound body-work prfrd.'

The future looked dark, indeed. Of course, every model would need a handbook to guide the new owner: 'Good early morning starter, but needs plenty of choke and revving in winter. Trained to bring morning tea, but won't wash up. If troubled with snoring, bang on bonnet or whistle in ear.'

'The sort of exchange ad. your mother might put out,' I
continued to the marbles player, 'is something she's had no
experience of, something like—"Wanted, model husband, good
gardener, handyman, do-it-yourself expert, sober and able to
carve. Bonus of 500 Green Shield stamps if equipped with
sound memory." '

At which a smile spread across her morning face. Ah, here
comes the thaw . . .

18. Sex and the Six O'Clock Kid

THE MARY WHITEHOUSES of the world complain constantly of the disturbing influence in the home of TV violence and sex. This isn't my problem at all. With my brood it seems to be so much water off a duck's back. They don't believe any of it.

Only the eight-year-old evinces what could be termed as a disturbing reaction. At the mere mention of the word 'bosom' —as there was once again while we sat viewing a Shakespeare play the other night—he rolls around the floor laughing hysterically. 'Bosoms! Bosoms!' he shrieked, then curled up in a paroxysm of mirth.

'Be quiet, I can't hear!' I said.

'But that man said "Bosoms"! Didn't you hear him? Bosoms!' And off he pealed again, rolling about the floor clutching his sides with helpless laughter. He finally rolled onto the dozing cat, who added her own squeal of protest and dived under the table.

I cannot interpret anything from this other than the faint possibility that when he grows up he could well be another legman, like his father.

No. TV sex is no real problem, but there are other disturbances which TV brings into the home and which Mrs White-house never talks about. It's time they got some of the spotlight.

Take the commercials. Those power-drill ads for a start. The third or fourth time he saw one on the box he turned to me and said, 'You haven't got a power-drill, have you?' I confessed that I hadn't and his lips curled up in disgust. I felt pretty uncomfortable.

A few days later the same lad came to me and said he had

to carve something for school and why didn't I have saws and tools and make things? 'You're not a real father at all!' he said angrily.

The shaft struck home. My trouble is that I come from a long line of non-do-it-yourselfers. Mention a screwdriver or a paintbrush and I want to go to sleep. I can't help it. The deep reason behind it all, I'm sure, is that things always go wrong when I try. From the first swing of a hammer I face the insurmountable. Half the wall falls down, or I get the only box of right-handed screws ever issued for left-handed holes, or the only paintbrush in the world suffering from galloping alopaecia. I could go on all day about do-it-yourself disasters. No wonder the word puts me to sleep.

However, clutching my wound, I went to some extraordinary lengths to scrounge a bit of wood from a builder and I carved a rough animal shape with the bread knife. I was just adding the finishing nick to the carving, and thinking that for once a do-it-yourself job had actually gone right, when the Chief Fairy saw what I was doing and leapt at me with a near-scream.

'That's the bread knife, you fool!' She grabbed it from my hand. 'It's not for cutting wood, you'll ruin it!'

I tell you, a *real* disturbance of the home followed and none of it would have happened if the innocent boy hadn't seen it on TV. *But Mrs Whitehouse worries about sex.*

Then came the telephone craze. Brainwashed by all the telephoning he sees on television, he demanded a birthday present of a home telephone he'd seen advertised. He gave us no peace till it was rigged up from his bedroom to the bedroom of his friend next door.

At 6 am every day the bells would start ringing. The first time it happened I staggered bog-eyed from bed, wondering who the devil was ringing at the door in the middle of the night. Then I heard the pint-sized communicators at it . . .

'Hello, is that you?' 'Yes, this is me. Is that you?' 'Yes, it's me.' 'Oh, well, good-bye then.' 'Good-bye!' 'Good-bye!' 'Good-bye!'

c*

Five seconds after the phone had been replaced the bells would start again . . . 'Hello, is that you . . .?'

Six weeks of bell-ringing and the telephone chatter at the crack of dawn. *But Mrs Whitehouse worries about sex.*

One day, thank God, the telephone batteries ran out and neither my neighbour nor I has dared to replace them.

Now he wants to be a child actor, like all the other kids eating cornflakes, beans, soup, ice-cream, chocolate and sailing Shredded Wheat canoes on TV. They're his new heroes. And what wild fiction this is! As one housewife wrote to me indignantly, 'Those perfect little TV darlings, eating, drinking, taking their medicine, so willingly and without complaint— not one of them needing to be prodded, pushed or yelled at! What sort of a dream world is this? Where have I gone wrong?'

Nowhere, madam. It's like those neat and tidy TV kitchens where every wife is smiling, gay, crisp and fresh, as though she's ready to step into a fashion parade. If you believe *that*, open your wardrobe door—there's a bank manager standing there.

However, to return to the brainwashed, frustrated actor, standing at four-feet-two-and-a-teacake. As a preliminary to his new ambition, he demanded that I fatten up his part in his school play, which was something of an ad-lib affair about a magic toy shop.

At last, I thought, I could come to the rescue with tools I knew something about. So I duly fattened up his part, throwing in a song or two. I gave him the script and he was delighted.

But came the day of the play and what happened? He dried up. He couldn't remember it. The part was too long, he said. And who got the blame? The scriptwriter.

And Mrs Whitehouse worries about sex.

19. Requiem for a Rabbit

THE POOR OLD RABBIT died the other day. Another emotional crisis, floods of tears and father again called on to conduct the funeral service.

I don't mind confessing I got a bit choked up myself, too. It's sad to see kids upset at the loss of a loved pet. You feel pretty helpless, but I suppose in its own way it teaches them something about the impermanence of life and the other side of the happiness coin.

It was 7 pm, pet-feeding time, when the girl came rushing in from the back. Her face was white, her lips trembling. 'I think Whiskers is dead,' she said. 'She's just lying there in her cage.'

There was a swift, concerted movement out through the kitchen to the back garden entrance where Whiskers was kept in her two-roomed cage, with friendly vantage views of visiting milkman, tradesmen and neighbouring kids, when she wasn't hopping about the garden.

'She always comes straight out to meet me when I bring her the cabbage and carrots,' the girl was saying urgently, 'but this time she didn't, and when I looked into the part where she sleeps she was just lying there, not moving.'

I opened the wooden door to the sleeping quarters. The group gathered anxiously behind me. Whiskers was lying strangely still on her side. I reached out, but I knew already. Her white fur was cold. 'Yes,' I said, 'she's dead.'

For a little while there was silence, then the tears came. The boy turned away to hide his. The rabbit had been only three years old, but that had been a third of the boy's life. 'Why did she die?' he said, his eyes wide and moist.

'I don't know, son,' I said. 'All animals have to die sometime.' Two years ago it had been Bubbles, the guinea pig, who now lies under the mulberry tree at the bottom of the garden, with a small twig cross to mark the spot.

The group returned sadly to the house, and a little while later I found the boy lying on his bed, curled up round the cat and stroking her head. Smokey's 11, which is kind of elderly for a cat.

Not that I think the boy had any immediate fears for Smokey. It's just that in times of stress, like the rest of the family, he likes to talk to her and stroke her. In the parlance of the very young, Smokey has a 'grey stroke'—against the 'white stroke' of Whiskers.

Smokey is also a very good listener, the perfect psychiatrist, in fact, who never leaps in with her own oar, but hears you out with soothing, sympathetic purrs. And there are things you can tell a cat that you'd never dream of telling people. I knew how the boy felt, and recalled my own agonies with pets when I, too, was a 10 year old.

There were the white mice that I kept in a box in my bedroom, until a growing and mighty pong revealed my secret to the household and they were banished to a back garden cage, where one night they all mysteriously vanished.

Then came the pigeons. It was a sudden, mad, love affair. I just had to own pigeons and I made a cage out of a tea chest and wire mesh. On my 11th birthday I went to the bird market and bought four pigeons for a shilling each. 'They're homing pigeons,' said the man at the stall. 'If you keep them in the cage for three days, feed them corn, then let them out, they'll fly round your house and come back to the cage.'

Of course, there's one born every minute, isn't there? After four days—one extra, to be sure—I let them out. They flew round the house all right—for about a minute. And never came back. They were all on sale again at the same market a week later.

So much for my love affair with pigeons. I bought a tortoise next. At least I'd be able to catch it and bring it back if it had similar ideas. But that, too, vanished from the garden one night. This was followed by a Chinese rat, a rabbit and a hedgehog, all of which passed over to that Great Big Menagerie in the Sky. So I know a bit about getting emotionally involved with pets.

Anyway, the day after Whiskers died I went out with the spade and dug another grave under the mulberry tree, beside the guinea pig's. The kids didn't want to come to the graveside, but they watched from the garden window as I laid Whiskers to rest.

I wondered whether I ought to say a few words over her, but all I could think of was 'Poor old Whiskers', so that's what I said and started sprinkling the soil on top.

The watching boy was clearly moved because the next thing I knew, he was standing to attention at the garden window, eyes moist again, playing the funeral march on his flute. It was deeply touching. A real requiem for a rabbit.

20. Conker-Time Syndrome

'OH LORDY, I'm really growing old,' she sighed, walking into the room and flopping onto the settee. 'Do you realise that in two weeks' time I'll be 13 . . .? *Thirteen!*' She repeated the figure in slow amazement. 'I'll actually be a teenager!'

The poor decrepit thing cupped her chin in her hands and stared disconsolately out of the garden window. Clearly senile decay was setting in. She needed comforting.

'Does the prospect appal you?' I said.

'Oh, I'll be all right, I suppose.' She shrugged. 'I don't *feel* any different but—I don't know, where's it all gone, the *time*, I mean? It seems only yesterday that I was 11.'

She watched a September leaf float down onto the rabbit hutch and I began to feel like Methuselah. I went to the bar to pour myself some cough mixture. I poured one for the Chief Fairy, too. We'd better start packing in some living, I thought, before it's too late.

But first the mood of nostalgia had to be dispelled. Was it the season, conker time, the hint of bonfires and fireworks in the air again? I was trying to recall if there was a father's guide book for bringing up daughters and, if so, what it said about this unprecedented leap into near-old age.

Landmarks in her life began to appear in my mind's eye—fairy teeth under the pillow, falling in love at nine—'Oh, I'm so happy I'm me,' she had sighed dreamily that day she'd received her first written proposal on lined exercise paper '*Dear Kristeen, I woud liek to kiss you. Will you marey me?—John.*' And now it was all behind her.

A teenager, eh?' I repeated and the emotive word hung

again in the autumn air like the threat of a dire plague. But she wasn't listening. She had gone to her record-player and was playing one of her oldies. The Seekers. They were a big hit when she was seven—God, a century ago.

Her eyes were misty as she listened. 'I loved that *Island of Dreams*,' she sighed. 'What a pity they all broke up.'

A small, sympathetic tear began to well up inside me for the Good Old Days of when she was seven. Why the devil did they have to go and break up? I took another gulp of cough mixture.

'You can hold my hamster for a while, Christine, if you like,' said her middle-aged brother of nine, who likewise had sensed that her childhood was vanishing for ever. 'And I won't charge you anything. You can have a free hold.'

I mean, God, it was enough to tear your heart out.

'Thank you, Gavin,' she said to her brother with a new, sad politeness which she doubtless felt was more in keeping with her advanced years. She took the animal on her knee, stroking it and quietly humming the last strains of her *Island of Dreams*.

It was all too much. The Chief Fairy gulped and proffered her glass for another pre-dinner drop of cough mixture. Her own eyes were misty—for what, I know not, but probably for the ghosts of memory lane, dolls' houses, baby dresses and summer sand castles.

It was time to call a halt before we all drowned in buckets of nostalgia, and anyway, I suddenly realised that I'd been here before. On her eighth birthday the same child had looked up from her pillow and said solemnly, 'Daddy, I'll never be seven again, will I? Ever.' I remember I felt quite depressed for her. It was obviously the conker-time syndrome, which, of course, is by no means exclusive to one age group of conker players, nor, in my case, restricted to September.

It seems to me that we all advance in a series of jerks, rather than growing older gradually. Birthdays may nudge us forward a year at a time but what really floodlights our personal egg-timers are those shattering moments that deal in time scales of five, ten and twenty years, or more. Months go by, you don't feel a day older, then Old Father Time pushes a news item under your nose which announces that some child pop star is forty. Forty? That *boy*! But surely, only the other day he was 24? My God, so how old are you? In one moment you advance decades with another blinding picture of the heap of sand at the bottom of your egg-timer.

'Yes, well,' I said, clearing my throat and determined to try to introduce a note of cheerfulness into all this nostalgic wallowing, 'being another year older, even at 13, isn't that important. Birthdays are purely an arbitrary division of the span we're allotted. In another couple of months I'll be a year older, too. Am I groaning about it?'

'It's not the same,' said the imminent teenager. 'When I have my birthday I'll be one twelfth older. Eight per cent older. You're only a fortieth or fiftieth or something small . . .'

'Oy! Oy! Watch it!' I was moved to say.

'Purely an arbitrary division,' murmured the Chief Fairy, sipping her cough mixture.

'And think of all the presents you'll get, Christine,' encouraged the old greybeard of nine. 'I've got a whole year to wait for mine. You can have yours in two weeks.'

'Yes, that's true,' she said, brightening. 'Still it's a bit sad to think I'll never be twelve again. Ever.'

'And your daddy will never be 32 again either,' said Madame. So I grabbed the last of the cough mixture.

21. St Denis the Menace

A NEW MENACE has crept into the Englishman's castle. It is more troublesome than a blocked drain, unpaid bill, overgrown lawn or even the boiled egg problem. It is called 'A Project', and all the fathers I know go pale when they hear the dreaded syllables.

Projects are designed by teachers to see just how dumb father is—and maybe, as a side-issue to see if his son or daughter is another chip off the old blockhead.

At least, that's the way it comes over to me. My kids bring projects into the house from school like they might bring in a toad or a snake, or anything else you want to stand well back from.

For the uninitiated, a project is an exercise in research which can take anything from days to weeks, dominate the conversation in the home, divert adult minds from essential tasks, interrupt business conferences and ruin the Sunday dinner.

'Find out all you can about . . .' the teacher instructs the class, then sits back no doubt contemplating with Machiavellian glee the effect on the home.

This is not to be confused, by the way, with the Newsbook, in which young children lay bare all your dark, domestic secrets through the school term and holidays, too. Here the parent is involved only to the extent that teacher's eyebrows shoot up at such items as, 'On holiday we stopped at a pub and daddy got tite,' or 'Mummy went swiming but couldn't get her nickers on on the beech so daddy held a towl up. She fell over.'

No, with the project it's different entirely. 'What do you

Another exclusive for the newsbook.

know about the standard forms of punishment in the 15th century, mum?' the child asks, slinging her satchel onto the kitchen table. Mum knows nothing. So they wait to pounce on father the moment he comes through the door.

It isn't that father doesn't want to help, it's the exposure of his ignorance he has trouble with. His wife could begin to doubt his infallibility and brilliance. 'Oh, I thought you'd know a thing like that,' she says off-handedly. 'You always said you did well in history . . .' See what I mean?

One father I know, in a desperate attempt to defend his position as the knowledgeable head of the house, is having a running argument with his son's master over the origin of Jutes. The son has become a mere go-between, a constant messenger of information dredged up from ancient reference books by a harassed dad who should be doing other things.

Dad thinks he's winning at the moment and is still treated with proper respect in his castle, but who knows what the master will dream up to hit him with next week?

When I say the menace is new I mean, of course, comparatively. In my day we had a simple thing called an essay. All you did with any given topic set as homework was kick off with 'There are many kinds of . . .', chew your pen for a bit, chunter on for a couple of pages, then reach for your skates.

But that's not good enough today. They want the stuff in depth, words, pictures and diagrams, reams of it; the inevitable result of a rat-race where a university degree has become a minimum requirement for a job.

Projects start when the kids are about eight years old and go on, as far as I can see, till they get married or fly the coop. Only then can dad, the doddering legman in the research team, take it easy. At least as a bonus he can baffle his friends in the saloon bar with his staggering knowledge of 15th-century punishments, the origin of Jutes, the love life of fish and other riveting topics.

But in the meantime he has to learn to live with it, preserving face in his family.

The other evening I was present at a conference when the telephone rang. The boss went pale as he listened. Had the firm been taken over? His shares dropped through the bottom of the market? His wife run off with the milkman?

Finally he cupped his hand over the mouthpiece and hissed to his assembled colleagues, 'Who was the patron saint of Paris?'

I recognised the symptom at once. The dreaded project had struck again.

'St Denis,' a colleague said confidently.

The boss sighed with relief. 'Ah, yes, it was St Denis,' he said into the phone, relaxed and beaming again. 'Okay, son?'

I looked at the man who'd given the right answer. That's something else we have to put up with in the project game. Insufferable swots and teachers' pets.

22. Beaucoup de Gob-Stoppers

I VENTURED INTO the Junior Common Market the other day with a bunch of experts on gob-stoppers, liquorice sticks and other items of vital interest to 11-minus minds. And I'm happy to report that all is well. Prices and quality are satisfyingly on a par with our own tuck shops.

But the adventure was not without its trials. Our expedition, 80 strong and sporting gay, red-bobbled, woollen caps for easy rounding up of boisterous strays, set sail from Folkestone to Boulogne under the guise of a school outing. At least, that's what our ten-year-old's headmaster called it, but we all knew the secret purpose : to test the froggy gob-stoppers and see whether Parliament had made the right decision.

The headmaster had invited Madame and me to join as parent-helpers, which we bravely did, and at the ungodly hour of 7 45 am, when the eyelids were hardly yet forced apart, we assembled in the school playground.

Each teacher and helper was handed a lunch bag and a bag of mixed children. Then off we set for France, where very quickly I ran into my first major problem. Something had gone wrong with my French. It had been too long in storage.

I'd got all the Gallic shrugs, the gestures, the expressive hands, the thrust of the eyebrows—all the Fernandel facial language, in fact—but nothing was coming out between the lips. At least, nothing intelligible.

It might impress one's small son as one grimaces and gestures across the breakfast table, throwing in the odd phrase with linguistic *bravura, 'Ça va, mon vieux? Eh? Alors! Tiens! Il fait beau, n'est pas? Aw! Hein!'* But of no use at all when the same small son grabs you in a Boulogne street market and says, 'Listen—ask this man if he's got any of those long, winding pieces of liquorice.'

All the eyebrow thrusting, shrugging and grimacing in the world isn't going to help. And it didn't. It's terrible to be exposed as a phoney like that. Slap in the middle of the Junior Common Market.

It was to the street market that we headed on arrival and the stall-holders must still be wondering what hit them. At one time it was like a scene from a Woody Allen film : 'Pardon, m'sieu, do you sell le ice-cream? Oui? Good, bon, I'll have 64, please.'

'Mon Dieu!'

'And Hilary and Susan and David, you want yours with chocolate, don't you? Anybody else for chocolate? Or raspberry?'

'Sacré bleu!'

Educationally, each child had to ask for something in French and within ten minutes 70 of them were waving trophies of French bread as well as chewing every imaginable French sweet. They descended on the shops like a horde of red-capped, satchel-swinging locusts, and left the *boulanger* and *bon bon* merchants agreeably stunned at the sudden rise in their sales graphs.

At this time we were also following some useful Junior Common Market notes, thoughtfully prepared for us by the headmaster and written with a keen eye for essentials. Item : Crossing roads—please cross at the *Passage à Pietons*. But do not assume that cars will stop for you.' Just like home.

From the market we climbed to the ramparts of Old Boulogne for our picnic in the autumn sun, where our presence drew the attention of several curious French youngsters. It turned out they wanted to try their English, which seemed to bode well for the Junior Common Market.

But one thing I couldn't help noticing on this pioneering expedition was the way individual character emerged in the course of the day's adventures—the helpless, the brave, the leaners, the independent and the accident-prone. All to-morrow's shoppers.

One such lad in my care, in the accident-prone group, whose satchel straps had broken, whose socks were round his ankles, whose market-bought grapes had been stood on, whose lemon-ade had been kicked over and for whom everything was clearly going to go wrong throughout life, presented at one stage a most heart-rending picture as he trailed his busted satchel and dripping string bag down Boulogne's main street to the ferry.

The dripping was obviously mystifying him and he kept stopping to examine himself. 'Sir,' he said plaintively, 'can you tell me where I'm leaking now?' It was typical of his extreme category of accident-proneness that there was nothing left in his bag to leak—*but he was leaking*.

Our expeditionary force finally got back to the school at 9 30 pm *très heureuse but fatigué*. And if I was still counting red-bobbled caps in my sleep, my day was made by the young accident-prone king. He stumbled up to me in the dark outside the school. 'Thank you for looking after me, sir,' he said. I got quite a lump in my throat.

Madame's day was made, too. As she flopped out in the house at the end of it all, she murmured dreamily, 'Marvellous. I've been called Miss for the first time in 20 years.'

23. Father's First Quickstep

SHE CAME INTO THE ROOM wearing pale blue trousers and a white jumper. 'How does this look, daddy?' she said. 'Do you think it's nice?'

'Smashing,' I said.

'Are you sure?'

'Positive.'

She looked at me doubtfully as I yawned and shifted the week-weary muscles on my Saturday afternoon couch. The book slipped from my hand, the eyelids drooped. Ten minutes later she was back. 'Or do you prefer this?' she said.

I jacked up the eyelids again. The trousers and jumper were back in the wardrobe. She was now wearing a blue midi.

'Smashing. Great,' I murmured. The eyelids clanged back.

'No! Which? Which do you prefer?'

'Either.' The voice was dozily slurred. The eyes were struggling against the jack again. 'Both mar'lous . . . sss . . .'

'Daddy!'

I groaned. Thirteen years old and you know who she takes after, don't you? What is this driving urge women have for jumping in and out of different clothes all the time? Is it something that comes down in the genes?

'All right. The trousers. Okay? The trousers, they're the best. Right?' I said. I suppose I should have sensed the warning signals then. There was just a mite more urgency in her eyes than there usually is when she seeks my approval of an outfit.

But I had other matters to attend to. I was playing in a friendly four-ball of world champions, me, Palmer, Nicklaus and Player, and turned back to my zizz to get on with the game. Just as I was about to hammer another 500-yard drive down the fairway, with the other three cringing in submission, I was prodded from behind on the 10th tee. She was back again.

'I've decided,' she said. 'What I'm going to wear is this.' She stood there in a mini. 'It's all right for a dance, daddy, isn't it?'

Dance? What dance? A small shot of adrenalin burst over the four-ball at the 10th and blasted them out of my dream. This was no time for golf.

'What do you mean, a dance? Where? When?' I said, sitting up and staring at her. She doesn't go to dances. She never goes to dances. She's only 13 (and never mind the superstitious bit).

It's only a teenage dance—what are you worrying about?

'It's tonight, in the village,' she said.

'But . . .' I rose and began to pace the room. I was oddly disturbed. This was a new one. 'But why a dance? I mean, what sort of a dance?' I said, somewhat lamely. 'Who's going?'

'It's a barn dance. Other girls from the school are going.'

Girls! Never mind the girls! A fresh horror struck me. 'Good lord, you're not going in *that,* are you?' I said, staring at her mini-skirt.

'Don't you like it?'

'Er, yes, of course, but . . . er, the midi, or, er, the trousers would be better, don't you think?' I noticed I was pacing the room a bit too fast. In fact, I was doing a very fast quickstep of my own. I slowed down just as the Chief Fairy came in. 'Here,' I said, switching my attack, 'do you know your daughter's going to a dance tonight?'

'Yes,' she said. 'What's wrong?'

'But . . .' I was floundering in this strange new trauma of fatherhood. 'I was 17 before I went to a dance.'

She eyed me drily. I thought for a moment she was going to pierce me with a comment about being a late developer, but all she said was, 'For heaven's sake, it's just a teenage barn dance in the church hall.'

The words 'church hall' suddenly had a soothing quality I never suspected. Yet even so it wasn't enough. All thoughts of rest or championship golf had gone for the day and at eight o'clock I drove her down to the church hall.

From the car I watched her buy her ticket and go in. I had the desperate feeling that something was going out of my life for ever. Music and laughing voices floated out through the hall entrance. Dammit, I just had to make a final check, so I got out of the car and peeked in through the door. And guess what I saw?

Dancing youngsters? Sure. But grouped in a corner of the hall a dozen or so fathers trying to look casual and disinterested —though watching like hawks before they withdrew. I wasn't alone with those first dance dithers.

24. Keeping Up with the Averages

MR AND MRS AVERAGE, according to another of those never-ending polls, spend 12 years watching television in their average viewing lives of 64 years.

I don't know about you but the activities of this fellow Average are beginning to bore me. He's a bit of a twit, actually. Anyone who spends 12 years watching the box and becomes the father of 2.6 kids has got to be a bit of a twit. That poor mite Point Six, why don't they get it seen to? If his boring father had spent fewer years snoring in front of the box and done something more constructive, the pathetic little thing might be all in one piece today.

But there you are, what can you expect of a fellow who's only got three-and-a-quarter suits in his wardrobe, reads one-and-a-half books a year, and keeps two-fifteenths of a dog and one-twelfth of a cat?

Why doesn't somebody send the RSPCA round to his two-and-a-quarter bed-roomed house? Those poor emaciated animals ought to be put out of their misery.

He really is the absolute end, this fellow Fred Average (his real name, of course, is Jack Smith, but the fact is that he finds it embarrassing when he books in at hotels with his 34-year-old wife for their four-and-seven-eighths nights a year, which only a fellow called Average would do).

There he stands in his 75p socks and his 28p haircut, thinking his average thoughts and doing his average thing, spending £1.25 each week on cigarettes, 75p on beer and working eight-and-a-half days for one firm and getting a fifth of a gold watch at the end of it. What a life! He never does anything different, does he? Either above average or below average. He permits himself seven-sixteenth of an affair when he's 38 and that's his lot. Everything is predictable.

He holidays in Bognor, Blackpool or other Spanish territories, sending home two-and-a-half 'Wish you were here' cards and tells everyone the weather was marvellous when it was coming down like stair-rods. He's out there on the roads today, too, in his four-fifteenths of a car.

As well as his 12 years' watching television (other figures by courtesy of Reid Opinion Poll Enterprises—or Old Rope for short), he spends 23 years in bed, 21 of them sleeping, two of them thinking, six days yawning, three days actually getting into and out of bed, and, give or take a cuddle or two, six months at the old nonsense. Not all at once, of course. Give him a chance.

This prize product of the polls has been so processed by the statisticians that he's not even real any more. No style, no panache, no flair—nothing. Just a dreary, middle-of-the-road stick-in-the-mud. And his 9st 5lb wife isn't much better. I mean, what kind of a numbskull is it who spends a year-and-a-half putting her face on, six months taking it off, two weeks pulling her tights on and walks 15 miles round her house every week?

Now then, what a nice change it would make if the market researchers and pollsters told us about Mr and Mrs Different. They must be in those statistics somewhere, if only to add some point to the lives of Mr and Mrs Fred Average.

Yes, let's take old Diff. I know for a fact that he doesn't always come home at 6 30 every night and get kissed two-and-a-half times a week by his wife—like Fred Average. Very often he rolls home at 5 30 am, smashed off his splendid head and singing with the dawn chorus. And with what he's been drinking not even his own mother would want to kiss him.

Neither would he dream of staying in one job for a fifth of a gold watch. Or, for that matter, have seven-sixteenths of a bit on the side at 38. It would be the whole bit or nothing. And more than likely he started at 17. But at least he's got a heart and he's kind to animals. He'd never keep two-fifteenths of a dog around the house. Not old Diff.

And he wouldn't watch television for two minutes, let alone 12 years.

However, if Fred Average is a dreary composite of Market research, there is at least one personality that the interminable opinion polls constantly refer to and who entertains me hugely. Have you noticed the onward shuffle of that dithering fellow, Don't Know? Indeed, in one recent poll on industrial relations he actually outnumbered those crisp men of decision, Yes and No.

It is fairly simple, of course, to see Mr Yes and Mr No in flesh and blood terms—clear-eyed, firm-striding, no-nonsense chaps who order their lives with authority and confidence, who always get served first at the bar, who know what we should do about Governments, foreign policies, equality for women and who's going to wash the dishes. But what of the private life of D. Know, Esq., who has seen his role in the world rendered down to a thin, doleful statistic in small percentages, who can never catch the barmaid's eye, who clearly lacks the mental robustness of Yes and No, but who is, nevertheless, a sensitive fellow? He has the misfortune to see all sides.

Consider his private agonies. Since he cannot make up his mind, each day puts him through torments of indecision from his first waking moments. 'Would you like bacon or boiled egg?' asks his wife, climbing out of bed, and D. Know, Esq., rolls over with a groan. His mind clams up and he pulls the blankets over his head.

His whole vocabulary is loaded with such phrases as 'On the one hand . . . but on the other . . .' Perched anxiously on the fence, he believes with Proust that all our final resolutions are made in a state of mind that is not going to last. And the day he got married was torture. 'Wilt thou take this woman . . .?' intoned the minister and his grey cells seized up in a sweat. This was no place for a Don't Know.

As the assembled congregation hung breathlessly on the silence, his lips fought to suppress the stock replies of compromise. 'I really have no strong feelings on the matter . . . Well, um, er, although there is much to be said for joining the "Yes" lobby, is there not also a case to be made out for the "Noes" . . .?'

Only the sudden steely glint in his bride's eye forced a decision from him. 'I will,' he gasped finally and the congregation breathed again.

Obviously, no portrait or Identikit picture of D. Know, Esq., would be complete without a personal description. His brow is furrowed with worry as befits a man of his wavering mind, and since he cannot come down on one side or the other he parts his hair in the middle. On the other hand, there are long periods when he prefers not to part it at all.

He wears old suits because he can never decide to buy a new one. Only his ties, shirts and socks change—every Christmas, since these are decisions of the Yes and No people in his life.

One moment though . . . there is something wrong here. What makes me think that D. Know is a man? I don't recall ever having seen his category in the polls broken down into sexes. And women are very good at not knowing, are they not?

What puts the thought in my mind is that I have at this very moment called out from my lonely eyrie to the kitchen below, 'What are we having for supper?'

'I don't know,' she said. 'What would you like?'

25. Make Mine Country Style

THERE'S NOTHING like a country holiday for putting the city man's life in perspective, for freshening his pipe-dreams, reminding him of what he's missing for nine-tenths of his life; and for rekindling his interest in his pools coupon.

It isn't only the pleasure of escape from the fume-filled, concrete canyons to the clean, wooded hills, dales, bird-song and wriggle of trout on line. Most of all the fleeing city dweller learns again the joy of greeting his fellow creatures.

In the city we become insulated against people. There are too many of us. Daily we pass each other in our teeming thousands without acknowledgement. It is in the country that we savour this joy again. I know. I have just savoured it.

Ambling down a sunlit lane one day recently I was hailed by an easy-going country fellow. 'Morning!' he sang out, with a friendly wave of his stick.

'Morning!' I called back. 'Lovely day.'

'Ah,' he said, cocking a weather eye upwards. 'Wind backin' up, though. Be rain later, I'spect.'

'Ah,' I said, slipping easily into the vernacular.

But can you imagine stopping in London's Strand to have that conversation? In the middle of the rat-race rush-hour you nod in friendly fashion to a chap, or even a mini-skirted typist, and say, 'Wind backin' up, eh?'

Things could turn very nasty. They'd have you run in.

The British have difficulty enough with their good mornings to strangers, a fact I can confirm after a recent encounter in my local park. I like to take an early morning stroll in this little oasis, usually round the duck pond, and recently I encountered another early morning walker.

At first we passed each other without even a glance, he with his head buried in his morning paper, I in some pools coupon dreamland. Thus insulated, we continued to pass each other for several mornings without any acknowledgement of the other's presence.

Then one day he appeared to observe me as he transferred his eye from the City section to the sports pages.

On succeeding days I noticed him stiffen a little as he became aware of the same fellow strolling towards him each morning. There were tentative, sidelong looks. We were, I should say, about the only people in the park at this hour and such a situation would be unthinkable in the country. It lasted two weeks. Then came the day of decision. I sensed it 50 yards away. There was a steadying of step, a shuffling of paper as an early eye was brought to bear on the approaching bird, a slight gritting of the jaw. I could almost feel the determination setting in.

A few yards from me he lowered his paper and looked me straight and challengingly in the eye. 'Morning!' he rapped out.

Despite myself I was caught a little on the hop. 'Morning!' I babbled back quickly.

He nodded and went on his way. It seemed to me that he was pleased with the encounter. He had got over what he clearly regarded as an obstacle on his morning walk.

But what he apparently forgot was that he would be meeting me again in a few minutes, on the other side of the circular pond. We rounded the bushes together, still marching in opposite directions.

For a moment his step faltered, but this time he kept his head down in his paper. Two good mornings to the same chap in one morning was clearly too much. Maybe, after all, this is why the city dweller doesn't acknowledge people easily. He knows there's a strong chance that he's going to be running into them all day long.

This, of course, is a problem we see constantly highlighted in offices. It seems a curious fact of life that people can be sitting at desks or typewriters and no one bothers about them, but the moment we are in locomotion somewhere, moving about corridors and passing people, we have to give some sign of acknowledgement.

The first time it happens in the course of a day it is no problem. 'Good morning!' we say. The next time we might reduce it to a nod, a smile, and perhaps a 'Hi!' or even 'Ho!'

Around about the fifth passing we have slashed through the whole ritual till we're down to a lift of an eyebrow. And by the time we've passed the same person ten times in the same corridor on the same day our eyes are searching for somewhere else to be. Which explains why you always find people walking down corridors with bits of paper in their hands. It gives them something else to look at, and they don't have to say good morning to it.

26. Roll on Thursday

MORE AND MORE I find myself looking forward to Thursdays. Not that I have anything against Tuesday or Wednesday or indeed any other day, except maybe Monday. But Thursdays are definitely tops at the moment.

That's the day my daughter does her cookery lessons in school and brings home the results.

Last week I enjoyed the most delicious macaroni cheese, the week before it was chocolate mousse, next week I'm promised rock cakes and the following week baked fish pie. All cooked in school and brought home in foil-wrapped dishes, ready for the taster's lips.

I'm the taster.

And before we proceed further, my compliments to the Cookery Mistress. I award the school five stars, my gourmet rosette and an A-plus. I'd throw in the Order of the Chrysanthemum, too, if I could.

All this, I'm sure, will come as good news to other fathers with young daughters who perhaps thought that all their offspring were learning in school these days were the three Rs and one S (and I don't mean Sewing).

The fact that cooking is being taught with such zest and style may owe something to George Meredith who wisely observed : 'Kissing don't last; cookery do !' He knew what the boy-girl scene was all about.

I must confess that I find it an entirely new and unexpected bonus of fatherhood. For my own daughter cookery started this term, and dealing with homework has become a real pleasure. Instead of being driven into a corner with the customary queries about Pythagoras and Latin declensions, I positively bounce out to help with Thursday's lessons. I'm supposed to be on a diet, but what sort of a mean father is it who wouldn't help his daughter with her school-work?

'Ah, spaghetti Bolognaise,' I drool through diet-strained lips. 'Let me see how you've done in school today.' And I set to with knife, fork and spoon, which I've had at the ready ever since she walked into the house. 'Very good. Very good indeed. Dee-licious!'

In my calorie-starved, semi-emaciated condition, perhaps it's little wonder that I've been giving her marks like 12 out of 10 and A-plus-plus-plus.

She is duly pleased. So am I. So is her younger brother, to whom I turn for a second opinion. 'Actually, this is pretty good, actually,' he is on record as saying, over a cheese and ham concoction. 'You're a very good cook, Christine.'

'You're darned right she is,' said I, munching happily, while the cookery pupil looked on with obvious pleasure.

'The pastry's not too flakey, is it?' she asked, tentatively. 'The teacher thought it might be, just a little bit.'

'It's absolutely perfect, beautifully done,' I replied. 'Wouldn't you say so, Gavin?'

'Absolutely, actually.'

'There you are. Twelve out of ten again, and never mind the teacher, we're correcting your homework, not her.'

All too soon the dish was scoffed, and fingers probed for the last crumbs.

But let me tell you of the biggest bonus to emerge from all this. The praise I have lavished has not gone unnoticed else-where, and though I would not for one moment suggest that any sense of rivalry has arisen in the happy home, I must reveal that all sorts of new and interesting dishes are now being offered to me by the Chief Fairy. Some of those million and a half hoarded recipes are actually reaching the table, actually.

Naturally, I make sure that I share my praise equally. I

know a good thing when I see it, and this is a very good thing indeed.

To be fair, she has always protested that there was little point in preparing delicate dishes for a meat-and-potato shower, but now it seems the *Cordon Bleu* of the Lower Fifth has released new taste buds in the family. And if a friendly feud should develop to satisfy them who am I to interfere?

Roll on Thursday, and if it's all right by the Cookery Mistress—any chance of some salmon *soufflé* next week?

Now it's Madame versus the Cordon Bleu of the Lower fifth.

27. Slap Happy Pappy

ONE THING a family man doesn't go short of these days is advice. Whatever else he's going short of, there's plenty of *that*.

Every day some expert sounds off on how he should run his marriage, his job, his kids, his home, his garden, his car, his secretary, his money, his body, his looks and his habits. In essence this advice amounts to : How to keep your wife happy, your boss happy, your kids happy, your home happy, your garden happy, your car happy, your bank manager happy and stay fit and gorgeous. Roll on ! What about slap-happy Pappy? Who's keeping *him* happy?

I admit that here and there amid the plethora of prescriptions for living that we get from our doctors, sociologists, accountants, beauticians and head-shrinkers, an occasional glint of sanity gleams from the headlines in our newspapers. 'Drinking beer improves the memory,' I thought, was a rather helpful recent one and went out of my way to draw my wife's attention to the article; as I did also with 'Mowing can deafen you, warns doctor.'

Of course, I have known for years of the damaging effect of lawn-mowing—or 'lawn-moaning', as one of my younger readers so delightfully described it recently—but it was nice to see medical backing for it.

My wife read the article, turned it over, examined it, held it up to the light and said it was a trick and who had I bribed to publish such canards? But it was absolutely genuine.

'Playing golf reduces heart attacks,' was also quite helpful counsel and so was 'Do-it-yourself men at greater risk in home accidents.' Used as a winning double they could take a screw-driver out of your hands and have a real driver in them on the first tee in no time at all—certainly quicker than she can say 'Will you put that curtain rail up?'

This is much more the sort of thing we beleaguered husbands could do with from the experts. So why don't we get it? One grows weary of hearing them knock all the fun out of living. Don't eat this, don't drink that, breathe in, breathe out, touch your toes, don't do this, that, or for heaven's sake the other, it'll weaken you or give you the screaming ab-dabs.

All the good things of life go on the banned list as illegal, immoral, fattening or giving you a fast ride to eternity. They've even infected the 11-minus bracket. Only the other day I heard of a small boy praying: 'Please God, make me a good boy—but not so good that I don't have any fun at all!' Infected or not, at least he had his priorities right.

So how fares the hectored husband amidst all this dismal advice?

I don't know about you, but I can tell you about me. I was sitting at home last week, wondering whether to get my ear muffs out and mow the lawn, or pop down to the local for a quick memory fortifier, when my eye caught this further piece of advice for us all: 'Put more fun into your wife's life and you'll live longer.'

Put more fun into your *wife*'s life! That takes the starch-free biscuit, I thought. The doctor who gave voice to that propaganda is either off his head or in the pay of the Women's Liberationists. Where is slap-happy Pappy supposed to find the time and energy after pleasing all the other experts trying to run his life?

Wasn't he recently being advised to put more fun into his secretary's life, take her out and entertain her? How about that for a fun day for his wife? 'Sorry, darling, I'll be late home tonight, I'm taking Miss Luscious out to the theatre, then supper, perhaps a nightclub and a nightcap or two . . . As long as I keep her happy.'

Oh yes, that would be a big hit in the happy homestead.

And what's his wife supposed to do? What's that? Develop new interests, new fun things? Oh, I see. FUN things. Now I'm with you, doctor . . . 'Here you are, darling, there's some terribly fun grass to mow out there. Borrow my ear muffs.' Next case.

28. Bubbles Speaking

I DON'T KNOW WHETHER I've been bending my ear in the wrong circles, but are nicknames dying out? Apart from those pop group labels like The Sink, The Toolshed, The Ballcock, or whatever, which deafen us daily, one hears few among the younger set.

Even the rising crop of Murphys, Millers and Wilsons that I know don't seem to be called Spud, Dusty and Tug any more. There wasn't even a Tug at No. 10. Is the fashion dead? This is Bubbles speaking, by the way.

For years they've been fading out in Parliament. They seemed to end about the time of Mac the Knife. And off-hand I can recall only Smartyboots Eccles and Churchill's dubbing of Selwyn Lloyd as 'Mr Celluloid'. What happened? Are people—and M.P.s—less chummy?

What started this particular ball whizzing round my mental pin-table was a remark I overheard from a woman writer the other day. She'd been nicknamed Jinx. 'My real name is Judy,' she said, 'but I was always doing things wrong, so everybody called me Jinx.'

Well, of course, the best nicknames owe their origin to personality or performance and most start in childhood. In my own school we had a fund of descriptive ones. From the masters alone I can still remember Stinker, Stoker, Featherbed, Paddy and 'Psst! *Cave*, here's Graniteface!'

All were built on some personality quirk and all were known to their owners in the Common Room. Though there was none quite so macabre as one recalled by a friend. He had a master named Death, whose wife was nicknamed Destruction. And their small son was known to the school as Death's Sting!

But now, of course, you're all waiting to hear how I came by my own. Though long ago discarded, I was nicknamed 'Bubbles' because as a small boy I had the great good fortune to be able to blow bubbles without any artificial aid, gum, pipe, blow ring or tin of soapy water. It was an amazing feat really.

I would sit in class astounding and hypnotising my friends with my great gift. All I did was curl my tongue in a secret way, moisten my lips and blow. And *olé*! Marble-sized bubbles would float down onto my exercise books.

The second form Remove would gaze in admiration and envy, even stupefaction. Sometimes one or two, in a jealous rage, would take their rulers and try to swipe them for four, or even six, as they floated inkwell-wards.

It was all a serious counter-attraction to any subject in the school curriculum. Mostly though, I remember, I did it in Paddy Lance's Latin class. Paddy was then about 96, short-sighted and near-deaf, poor chap. He was a kindly, white-haired leprechaun of a fellow, who shuffled about in carpet slippers.

If you sat anywhere behind the first two rows you could get away with murder, as well as bubble-blowing. Indeed, one lad, Smudger Smith I think it was, used to light up regularly in the back row.

'Is something burning?' Paddy asked once, his hairy nostrils twitching. And he began to shuffle down the lines of desks.

There was a suppressed titter as Smudger madly flapped his copy of Virgil, trying to disperse the great cloud of smoke rising over his desk.

Paddy's peering eyes finally homed in and narrowed on him. 'Are you *smoking*, boy?' he demanded.

'No sir, not me, sir,' panted Smudger, screwing the cigarette butt under his heel. 'I think it's the gardener's fire outside, sir. Shall I close the window, sir?'

Paddy peered closer at him, his nostrils still twitching. 'Very well, boy,' he nodded after a moment and Smudger jumped up like a frog with hot foot and banged the window up and down. It was, of course, already shut, but poor old Paddy couldn't see.

I remember the day well because it was the same day I thought my bubble-blowing gift had deserted me. I was panic-stricken. I couldn't get the fuel onto the launching pad. I was working my lips madly, staring with concentration into the mid-distance when Paddy sneaked up on me in his slippers.

'Are you all right, Reid?' he frowned.

'Sir?' I gulped, snapping down the launching pad.

'You're not feeling sick, boy, are you?'

'No, sir, not me, sir.'

Sick? Only at the thought of losing my precious gift. However, it turned out that the injection fuel had been temporarily ruined by bubble-gum.

Of course, I kicked the habit a long time ago. I'm no longer known as 'Bubbles'. My friends call me other names.

D*

29. Pinning Your Ears Back

FALL IN the shirt disposal unit! We are about to defuse, disarm and dismantle one of the most lethal anti-personnel weapons ever to find its way into modern man's wardrobe—the Mark I seven-pinned new shirt . . . Platoon ready, Cap'n.

(Come in John Wayne; no one else can play the role.)

Thanks, sarje. At ease, men. Now lissen you guys, let's git one thing straight. From here on it's gonna be tough. I only want volunteers in this man's army. Any guy feelin' queasy about the job we gotta do, or don't like the sighta blood, can fall out now and won't be disgraced none. Okay, men? Right . . .

Thanks, fellers. Kinda noo I could count on ya.

First off, men, lemme give ya the battle picture. We're in the hot area of this here war. Whoever dreamed up the blood-thirsty notion of minin' a guy's noo shirts with pins I don't know—maybe the same evil lunkhead who invented limpet mines, Molotov cocktails and boobytrap beds with bombs in 'em—but one thing's for sure, men, it's *us* the enemy's out to git.

Shirts are comin' at us armed to the teeth. The enemy don't bother to sabotage dames' knickers or blouses or dresses. It's the shirt-wearers he's aimin' at. One slip and you gotta hunka shirt shrapnel lodged in your mitt or your neck.

I don't wanna shoot you guys no line, but you gotta know the true picture *(faces turn pale as the Captain strips off his shirt to show the sticking plaster patches all over his back; he holds up his pin-scarred hands)* . . . Yeah, I know it's not a pretty sight, but it was my boithday yesterday and I got four noo shirts.

These here scars mark campaigns with the drip-dry armies of the shirt-makers. When the enemy gets into ya wardrobe he means WARdrobe.

Now what we got, men, is 34 shoppin' days to the great shirt bombardment of December 25, when the enemy's amm'nition is gonna explode in our Christmas stockin's. Casualties are

Look out for that shrapnel, sarge—one slip and Pow!

gonna litter the battlefield unless we do sumpin about it and show the free world how to deal with all this goddam shirt shrapnel. So let's git to battle stations, men, with that little parcel out there, a ribbon-cord, drip-dry, seven-pinned lulu. Size 16½. On ya hands and knees, men! Follow me!

First off, we remove the box. Right? Now snip the transparent outer casing and slowly draw it off. Easy now, you can slice your fingers off on this stuff. You gonna need all your blood for the big attack.

Right? Now shake the shirt out. Heads down! Quiet! Okay now—*slowly*. Feel for the locking clips on the shoulders . . . here, take over sarje, hand me the sweat rag . . . Okay? Got 'em, sarje? Right, gently withdraw 'em, one by one . . . Gently, I said! Okay, steady now, pins are right and left of ya there . . . great work, sarje. Now for the collar . . .

You gotta remove this plastic scaffolding around the collar

to git at the neck pins. Okay Sarje? Out they come . . . Swell!
We're doin' swell, fellers, let's take a breather. Hand me the
rye, Mac.

Okay, here we go then and hold your breath. Turn the
shirt over. Easy does it now. Pull the cardboard central casing
out, sarje . . . It's stuck? It's . . . *the arm pins, you fool*! It's
locked to the arm pins! You wanna rip your arm off? Stand
back! . . . Whew! Okay, sarje, take it easy, try again . . .

Okay, okay, you got those out now. Unfold the shirt. Easy,
boy, easy does it there's three more pins in the back, buried
deep . . . good, great. Swell work, sarje. A neat job. Let's
just run the magnet over it . . .

Yeah, That's it, fellers. This shirt has now been defused
and I can safely put it on and tuck it in like T-H-I-S!
EEEEaaaaow! You missed one! They got me in the shirt tail!

30. Upstairs, Downstairs

I AM GROWING somewhat disturbed by a strange compulsion my wife has developed for leaving things on stairs. These are things, apparently, which are downstairs and should be upstairs; and things also which are upstairs that should be downstairs.

To those of you already nodding to yourselves, 'Ah, poor chap, the strain got too much. He'd been married a long time, hadn't he?'—and looking round for the men in white coats to carry me off gibbering—I say wait!

In a moment all will become clear. At least I hope it will, though bachelors, bungalow-dwellers and anyone else living a one-level life may find it more difficult.

The fact is that, working from home recently, I became aware that at certain stages in the day the staircase seemed almost impassable and the way to my den blocked by all manner of clutter. This domestic fall-out began to mount on the third step from the bottom from about 9 am onwards. Peak-loading time seemed to arrive about 10 30 am, by which hour the Chief Fairy had done her morning whisking around downstairs and was thinking of starting upstairs.

At this time, on an average day's count, there were, piled on the staircase, the following : one concertina, one Monopoly set, one pullover, one pair of pyjama bottoms (small size), assorted tin soldiers and wheeled toys, one tube of new toothpaste, one new roll of loo paper, and one money-box policeman with a hole in his head.

How I became aware of this clutter is quite simple. I damned near broke my neck on it.

Wandering slowly downstairs from my room, hand on the rail, head thrown back for the inspiration that was eluding me in the work upon which I was engaged, I put my foot right in it—the third stair booby-trap, I mean.

My right heel shot off on a rapid ride on the bonnet of a toy jeep, my left knee, taken by surprise at this sudden desertion of a shared duty, buckled under the excess weight and only by amazing agility and presence of mind in holding on to the stair rail did I survive to tell this tale.

'My God, what are you trying to do—kill me!' I yelled.

Hearing the commotion, the Chief Fairy rushed from the kitchen for a ringside seat.

'What the devil's all this lethal clutter on the stairs?' I demanded, rising from the debris and clutching a wounded lower cheek, the target of a flattened toy soldier, with bayonet. 'I could have broken my neck!'

Of course, the moment she saw that I hadn't been killed, only slightly bayoneted in the rear, she began to do her falling about act, presumably on the basis that anything is funny provided it happens to somebody else. I quickly stopped that lot.

'Well, what do you expect?' she retorted. 'If you carried some of it up with you when you went upstairs you wouldn't fall over it!'

'What do you mean, carry it upstairs?' I retorted back.

'Do you think I put it there for decoration?' she flared. 'I put it there in the vain hope, after clearing up after you lot, that one day someone might actually take some of it back upstairs with them!' She was certainly warming to her subject and if I was looking for sympathy I wasn't getting any. Open one chink of your armour and they're in—pow!

She was amazed, she said, not only at me but the whole family in this matter. Every day the kids came in and dropped their satchels, jackets, hats and shoes all over the floor. They'd bring stuff from upstairs to downstairs and downstairs to upstairs, but the moment she—the Chief Fairy—put any stuff on the stairs every member of the family walked round it, or over it. No one ever dreamed of picking it up and taking it back to its proper home.

'They'll even say as they're walking round it or over it,' she fumed on, ' "You shouldn't leave that stuff there, mum, it's dangerous! Somebody might fall over it!" It could stay there for months and nobody would do anything about it!'

The way she was going on I half began to wish I'd only broken my neck. I turned and sneaked quietly back upstairs, carefully avoiding the hammer, scissors and sticking plaster on the top stair.

31. Socking the Great Cosmic Plan

'Why is it,' she hissed, as we stood temporarily alone at the cocktail party, 'that you always manage to introduce me to someone the moment I've put a sausage in my mouth?'

There was a slightly pained, aggrieved plea in her eyes as she said it, which was perhaps understandable. A moment before she had been compelled to juggle with her sherry glass, her handbag and a naked sausage stick in order to shake someone's hand. The cocktail sausage had just been popped into her mouth.

'Ah, you haven't met Harry, have you?' I said, introducing them quickly in the crowded room.

She stared wildly at Harry, then glared at me. 'How goo . . . er . . . how goo you goo?' she gulped madly, switching the sherry glass to her handbag hand.

'I goo very well, thank you,' Harry said cheerfully, taking her hand, but withdrawing it rather rapidly as the sausage stick jabbed his thumb. 'Ouch!' he winced, the smile and the wit vanishing in a flash.

'Oh, I'm terribly sorry,' she exclaimed, concerned and somewhat flustered, 'I was looking for somewhere to put it.'

Harry backed away sharply. 'It's all right. Really,' he muttered, striving manfully to smother the wince with a smile, a most interesting expression. Madame glared at me again.

Now I take this scene from a recent evening out, not because I wish to discuss the hazards of party-going, or the belief that my wife may have that I spend my life lying in wait for her to encumber herself with handbags, sausage sticks and sherry glasses, so that I can leap in with an introduction at the height

Another cocktail party calamity—another cosmic mystery.

of her calamity-proneness. No. All I want to know is: what the heck has it all to do with the great cosmic plan?

More and more I grow convinced that we're all on tramlines. All of us. Even this very moment, as you sit/stand/lie reading these words, was inevitable. There was no escape.

Think about it for a moment while I adjust my pop philosophy hat, pour myself another beer and contemplate man and his predicament from this rather comfortable garden chair (my own tram, temporarily resting in the garden, has decided it will mow the lawn later—much later).

I am aware that some readers may well have hurled this book from them by now, declaring, 'I'll fox him. I'll read no further and prove that I have free will.' That is the point where their own tramlines diverged fractionally from yours. But they are still on tramlines. Their points were programmed. Wave to them, folks.

In a word, or several, you are where you are, doing what you are because of who you are and where you came from. If you now decide to make a change because you're fed up with your particular tram ride, bully for you, but that was programmed, too. Character is destiny and destiny character. They are inextricably linked and were formed, some would say, at conception. I would go even farther back—back, in fact, to the cosmic conception. The Big, as it were, Bang.

You don't have to believe any of this, of course, but I do. At least I think I do. The evidence for it seems overwhelming—if only for the fact that things rarely happen the way you want them, or expect them, to. The unexpected always comes along to alter them. And the booming business of astrology suggests that more and more people want to sneak a look at their own blueprint for tomorrow.

But my point is : where does all the minutiae of life fit into the great universal jig-saw? Why do I waste so much time every morning trying to decide whether I'm putting my socks on inside out or not? What is the cosmic *point* of the dilemma?

There I sit, on the edge of the bed, poring over a sock heel, searching for a telltale bit of wool or nylon which will reveal the answer, but what has it got to do with the blueprint for the cosmos? And the cocktail sausage sticks, what about *them*? Sure, Harry goes around shaking hands more carefully these days and my wife has gone off sausages a bit, but to what ultimate end?

I can understand the cross-fertilisation of ideas where even the humblest thinker can pass on a small truth, which in turn influences another, which in turn . . . until one day man lands on the Moon. But where do my socks and the sausage sticks fit in?

One thing, though; not all life is completely unpredictable. The expected voice has just hailed my tram from the kitchen : 'Are you going to mow that lawn today, or not?'

32. How a Woman Thinks

WITH THE ONWARD MARCH of Women's lib., more and more key positions in the nation's affairs are falling to petticoat power. More and more women's minds are taking over from men's minds. Which brings us urgently to the new role of feminine logic in our all-equal, all-chaps-together society. And a right little minefield *this* is going to be.

Apart from the celebrated difference between men and women—which I do hope they keep—woman also differs from man in her 'thinks' bubbles. It is these bubbles I am about to examine. Yes, I am aware that it may seem a gross impertinence on the part of a male to attempt to explain what goes on in a woman's mind when half the time she doesn't know herself (as Cervantes remarked with bafflement, 'Between a woman's "yes" and "no" I would not venture to stick a pin.' Neither would *she*). However, on with the impertinence.

Much of man's bewilderment at the apparent illogicality of feminine logic arises from his failure to understand the process. It does not proceed like a mathematical theorem in the way of a man's. His own reason is based on an intellectual assessment of the evidence before him; a woman's on her emotional response to it, even if that response is in direct contradiction to the evidence.

This is why a woman reasoning with facts is such an awesome sight to behold. To her, facts quickly become people— or rather they represent a sort of reeded-glass window through which she peers to see who's in the bath. She will then step back, multiply two by two and announce triumphantly that the answer is 63. 'It stands to *reason*,' she will then have the apparent nerve to declare. Little wonder that strong men quail before it.

EXAMPLE : She burns the breakfast toast. The evidence shows that she left it under the grill too long. She forgot it. *Ergo* : It's *your* fault, because you didn't put the car away in the garage last night as she asked you to.

You're asleep in bed, but *you* burned the toast, Buster! It stands to reason.

Philosophers have pointed out before that the fundamental fault of the female character is that it has no sense of justice. Something is fair or not fair according to how she views the parties involved, regardless of the facts, and there's no knowing or predicting which way she'll jump. It is because the emotional factor is so strong and so variable in feminine logic that it produces the somersaulting decisions that bewilder men. This is the wild joker in the pack with whom *he* is trying to play a straight game of cards.

EXAMPLE : You both decide to go to a party to talk to other people for a change. At the end of the party she complains: '*You* didn't talk to me all night—you talked to other people!'

It is, of course, no use arguing that *that* was the object of the exercise, but if you're lucky you could escape the full blame. Feminine logic ruefully recognises that she could have been wearing her 'nothing-good-ever-happens-to-me-in this' dress.

Every man could compile his own list of woman's mind-blowing illogicalities, and no doubt has already done so. To a woman it is perfectly logical to have total recall of the cocktail chatter and who was wearing what at the last party, but to have no notion at all of the simple street directions to get there. To a woman it is perfectly logical to tidy up the house for the arrival of the daily cleaner, whose job it is to tidy up the house. To a woman, a car is a super car, not because it's well-built but because it's a blue one.

It is also logical for her to keep her husband's clothes clean, but not his shoes. The same man should always remember her birthday, but never add them up. Then again, bring her flowers when it's *not* her birthday and you're in dead trouble. Prepare for the inquisition. (This, of course, is *wife* logic at work, rather than *woman* logic—and the difference would require a whole book to explain.)

However, it would be wrong to suggest that all feminine logic is wildly out of touch with reality. It is not. It can be particularly effective where human relationships are concerned. Many a husband has ignored his wife's warning against the untrustworthiness of a new acquaintance or colleague, only to regret it later. Conversely, somebody whom he suspects could well find approval in the eyes of a wife, and again she often turns out to have made the right assessment.

Challenged to explain or justify her decisions, the woman might well be unable to do so. At the most she might put it down to the way the person in question holds his knife and fork. In the eyes of masculine logic, this, as Euclid observed, is absurd. But women are great readers of the small signs which men so often miss in their conduct of affairs with other men. Women's antennae are constantly active, registering the tiniest details of voice inflections, gestures, body movements and postures which can be so revealing. All the time they listen with their eyes.

Perhaps to a man, the most bewildering example of feminine logic at work is when his wife buys him, say, two ties and waits to see what he does. Fashion has not yet reached the point where a fellow may wear two ties and not be noticed, so he plumps for one tie—he has no choice. Then comes the inevitable exchange:

'Oh, so you don't like the other tie?'

'I think they're both very nice, but I can't wear two.'

'But that's the one you chose. What's wrong with the other one?'

That's *real* feminine logic at work. Yet in a way there is a grain of sense in it. By selecting two different ties she is unconsciously choosing two differing aspects of his personality, which she wishes to bring out. The dilemma forces him to reject one and she wants to know why. At least, that's *my* theory, although she probably did it by intuition, which is the other wild card in her personal pack.

A woman's intuition, one cynic noted, is the result of millions of years of not thinking. It is the factor that constantly flies in the face of the facts, but it led Chazal to declare: 'Men are cleverer than women at reasoning, women are cleverer at drawing conclusions. A Parliament in which the members were predominantly women would get through its legislation much faster.'

This, I am sure, is true. However, speaking as a husband, there is one aspect of feminine illogicality which still baffles me. It is bargain logic—by which she spends money to save it on something she'll never wear. I think it has something to do with that emotional joker in the pack. Excitement at the thought of a bargain dress, say at £10 instead of £30, blinds her to the fact that deep down she doesn't really like the darned thing.

This gives rise to the constant cry of women staring into a wardrobe full of clothes. 'I haven't a thing to wear.' (Note the difference in a man's wardrobe, where the few well-worn suits are worked to death.)

Never mind, in spite of their illogicality, what would we do without them? As the French philosopher Gourmont put it: 'What is truly indispensable for the conduct of life has been taught us by women—the small rules of courtesy, the actions that win us the warmth or deference of others, the words that assure us a welcome; the attitudes that must be varied to mesh with character or situation; all social strategy. It is listening to women that teaches us to speak to men.'

If we can get a word in edgeways, that is.

33. The Cordon Blur Cook

I DON'T KNOW WHETHER it's some sort of off-shoot of unisex, but have you noticed the growing male invasion of the kitchen? You can hardly turn a printed page these days without some chap boasting about his soup or his *coq au vin*, or his *shish-kebab*.

If he's not actually writing about it, or producing a cook book, he's leaning back on his after-dinner brandy talking about it. 'Did it on my infra-red spit, old man.' My infra-red spit, notice, not his wife's. Holy role reversal!

A lot of it also seems to smack of those wartime exploits. 'There I was, old man, with the gas on half-throttle, three onions on the starboard bow and two carrots below. What was I to do? Mince them or hurl 'em in whole?'

I don't know that I care for the trend myself. However, I suppose you've either got green fingers for this sort of thing or you haven't. I haven't. I'm more of your cordon blur, actually.

But don't think I haven't tried and what you are about to read are the untold secrets of My Cooking Career.

The first thing I ever cooked was a baked potato in a Guy Fawkes' bonfire. Everybody else's came out steamingly succulent and done to a turn. Mine was burned to a cinder outside and raw as old boots inside. Nine years old and already the writing was on the kitchen wall.

As I stood and examined it, pierced on the end of a twig, the truth came to me in a flash. All my life I was going to get the uncookable potato, the unboilable egg and the stubborn sausage that would split its insides out rather than yield to the coaxing of my pan. Like non-do-it-yourself men, it's the way we come out of the mould.

There and then I abandoned My Cooking Career, apart from one brief adventure with some porridge at a Boy Scouts' camp on the banks of Loch Ness. The result was hurled uneaten into the loch and it has been no surprise to me that the Monster has never been seen since.

But the greatest challenge was yet to come. I joined the Royal Navy and the second day aboard my first ship, a destroyer, I was told it was my turn to be 'cook of the mess' for the day.

'What does *that* mean?' I said, aghast.

'You peel the spuds, prepare the meat and take it along to the chef in the galley. Oh, yes, and do a figgy duff for afters,' said the leading hand of the mess.

Figgy duff? Me make figgy duff? This was the great naval dish concocted of flour and suet and water and raisins and Lord knows what else. I wanted to shout that I was only 18, confess about the baked potato and the Loch Ness porridge, but there was no escape. I had to make a figgy duff.

No one told you *how* to make it, of course—since it was the Navy's favourite pudding you were just supposed to divine the method by instinct, hazel twig or something. So all the forenoon, on a heaving sea, I slapped and pounded the goo across the mess-deck table, throwing in suet and raisins, and eventually bore it to the ship's galley in trepidation. Should I jump overboard now? Or wait to be keelhauled?

When the bosun's mate piped 'Hands to Dinner' I couldn't eat. I just sat watching Number Five mess chewing non-committally through the first course. 'Right, let's have the figgy duff,' said the leading hand, pushing his dinner plate away. I began to carve chunks off and pass them around. It seemed to resist the knife.

'Didn't you do no custard then?' demanded a three-badge A.B. I could only gulp and shake my head. I was too busy watching Knocker White, a torpedoman, as he sank his teeth into it. His mouth came away but his teeth remained in it.

'Gawd!' he cried, rescuing his choppers from the claggy, leaden, off-white goo on his plate. 'Oo made the bleedin' figgy?'

He spotted me cowering at the end of the table. 'Gawd! What did you put in it, mate? Bleedin' cement?'

All round the mess-deck table plates were being pushed away, and the expressions on the faces of the diners remain with me still. Only one man, an iron-stomached Ulsterman, chewed his way through the lot. 'Varry guid figgy, Callan,' he said in his ripe Belfast accent. 'Varry guid indeed.'

I thanked him for the compliment, but it was the one and only figgy duff they let me cook. When I threw the rest of the uneaten dollops of goo over the side, even the seagulls wheeled away in disgust. They knew the truth, too.

34. Stag at Bay

WHILE JOKING for years about the bra-burning Women's Libbers, have I allowed their insidious message to sneak in through my own back door? I could be wrong but I'm sure I detect a mood of derisive rebellion beneath the surface of the marital home. I think my authority is being challenged.

It's nothing I can put my finger on exactly, it's more of an uncomfortable feeling—a bit like the day the liftman doesn't smile at you and that's the day you get fired. I think there's a kitchen *coup d'etat* in the air.

The other night, for instance, right out of the blue, when I thought she was engrossed in a TV play, she burst out: 'Why is it always birds and dollies and dolly-birds and bits of crackling and crumpet and pieces of homework when men talk of women? We never speak of men like that. We don't say "There's a nice bit of muffin or bacon rind." Why can't men refer to us properly, as girls or women?'

Let me say at once that I had said nothing, absolutely nothing, to provoke this attack. I, too, had been engrossed in the play. And so taken by surprise was I that the outburst left me stunned and bereft of articulate reply.

While I groped my way up the ropes, lips opening and closing codwise, she hit me again: 'The same goes for wives, too. It's always the ball-and-chain or the trouble-and-strife or the little woman or the hired hand or the white man's burden. We don't call you names like that. We wouldn't be so insulting. Why do you do it?'

Let me repeat, I had said abso-bally-lutely nothing to bring on this assault. But at the count of nine I rose to my feet, groggy, yes, but beaten, no, and I said : 'Listen you—you Chief Fairy. Why pick on me? What did I do?'

'Sssh, be quiet,' she said impatiently. 'Never mind. Watch the play.'

Just like that—never mind, watch the play. How can you win?

But if that was a straw in the wind, on Saturday morning she hit me with the full haystack. At breakfast I had been riffling through my mail and had made certain announcements about my movements the following week.

'You're doing *what* on Wednesday?' she said, feigning, I thought, amused astonishment.

'Attending a golf dinner.'

'No, it was something else you said about it.'

'A stag do, I said it was.'

'That's it!' She began to fall about the breakfast table. 'A stag do! Ha-ha! A stag do!'

The kids, mystified but scenting a new assault on the patriarchal ramparts, perked up over their sharp-end-up boiled eggs. 'What's a stag do?' asked the youngest. At which his mother pealed off into more laughter. The image was too much for her.

'Well, it's all these stags, you see, son. Not real stags, of course, with fine heads and antlers and graceful bodies, standing on mountain tops and looking proud and courageous. It's these men like daddy who call themselves stags. Stags!' She shrieked off again—there was no holding her this morning. 'Short, fat stags, bald-headed stags, podgy, pot-bellied stags, all standing at the bar drinking and slapping each other on the back.'

She was shaking with mirth over her flat-end-up egg. The small son, still mystified, looked at me—or rather my head. I think he half expected to see antlers spring out of it by some magic.

In retaliation, I tapped my temple and shook my head at him knowingly. But she looked at me with blatant insubordination and said, 'All these brave stags, you see, like to feel they're on a mountain top, way up away from their wives. Very noble. If women do it, of course, it's different, it's a hen party. You see the subtle difference—men go to stag dinners to exchange important thoughts. Women go to hen parties to cackle. Right?'

I felt like the Stag at Bay and flicked my gaze out of the kitchen window. Smoke was curling up from an autumn garden fire. At least, I supposed that's what it was, but the way things were going she could have thrown all her bras on it, too . . .

And, of course, the next problem you face as a non-antlered, cotton-pickin' stag is how to sneak into your house and bed at 3 am without waking your lady-mate who expected you home at 11 30.

Home is the stag—on his hands and knees.
Where else?

One thing's certain, she won't be laughing when she wakes up. Which is why Stag at Bay is now very much Stag on Tipsy-toesies—and I do mean *tipsy*-toesies. The wine and brandy have taken their toll at the golf dinner.

Softly, softly is the message. Step on a creaking stair, twang a noisy bedspring and the stag will not only get a blast from his doe, he'll get it from her rae-me-fah-so-la-ti, too. And here let me pass on a few tips to other stags who will face this problem many times in their marriage:

Never undertake any task you think you might not accomplish. If you think you'll fall over while taking your shoes off, sit down. Lie down, even.

If you keep tip-toeing up three stairs and coming down four, face the fact that you'll never make the bedroom. Get down on your hands and knees. And don't keep whispering 'Ssshhh!' to the dog—he's only watching.

Undoubtedly, the most hazardous area to negotiate is that between the bedroom door and your side of the bed, mainly because it's all in darkness and alcohol has refracted your judgment of where all the obstacles are. Near-permanent bruises on my knee caps testify to my own inability to estimate where the corner of the bed is. I have even accused her of moving the bed on my stag nights just for the joy of hearing my knee-caps crack. However, should you stumble, do beware of what you grab hold of to steady yourself. This is vital.

There was the sad case reported recently of a returning stag who made the top of the stairs after four attempts—all the while shushing his silently watching dog—only to be defeated inside the bedroom.

He hung onto the wardrobe door for support. It promptly swung open and he fell inside. So his wife climbed out of bed, calmly closed the wardrobe door on him and got back into bed.

That's the sort of thing you've got to watch. All the earlier noise-avoidance precautions, removing shoes, wrapping up small change in handkerchief, turning bedroom door handle with delicacy of safe-cracker—all these can go for nothing in one unthinking moment.

There is also a certain type of bedroom stag hunter who stalks her quarry every bit as warily as the stag tries to evade detection. I have one. Just when I think I've made it, without creaking a floorboard or twanging a bedspring or getting my pyjamas on back to front—just when I think success is mine, the eggs hit the fan. She's been watching me from the moment I crawled into the bedroom on my hands and knees.

And let me tell you that the effect of a sudden brisk remark rapped out in the dark after all the tense silence can be traumatic. It happened the other day. As I was easing myself backwards between the sheets the voice cracked out of the gloom: 'What do you think you're playing at?' It was like a claymore between the shoulder blades.

In such a moment what can you say? In the early years you could have got away with blaming all your pals. It was Jack, or Jimmy, or Joe. But not now. She doesn't believe it. In fact, she's positively cynical about it—'You mean they *pounced* on you and *chained* you to the bar and wouldn't let you go?'

You've also been through all the other wild excuses . . . 'Suddenly everything went blank, honestly, darling. I never really believed in this loss of memory thing before but, so help me, six hours later there I was, turning the key in the front door and the church clock striking three . . . It was amazing.'

So with the claymore between my shoulder blades, what were my last words? 'I think,' I gasped, 'it's got something to do with putting the clocks back. I'm all confused.'

Oh boy, wait till the women have to start making the excuses.

35. Twang! Slurp! Yodellayeedee!

Now THEN, any reader of a nervous or excitable disposition is advised to switch off here or turn back to quieter corners on another page. This warning is given in view of the inflammatory nature of the subject matter the writer wishes to discuss here, namely women's suspenders.

From this point the author cannot be responsible for attacks of apoplexy, nervous dementia, frothing at the mouth, glazed eyeballs, hysteria or the screaming heeby-jeebies.

Not only is the author going to discuss women's suspenders and important matters pertaining thereto but he will be drinking martinis while so doing. Right? And he may also, this being at the time of writing, the festive season, break into a yodel or two. Okay? (Critics please note that with one burst of grapeshot you are now getting wine, women and song.)

Right, then, on with the suspenders, yodellayeedee!

By suspenders, of course—and let us get our definitions right for the benefit of our younger readers—I mean those little strips of material, black, white, blue, etc., that provide the gay bridge between a woman's stocking tops and what goes on underneath, on top. Slurp.

They are practical, efficient, decorative, adaptable and adorable. Slurp.

But most of all, they add a new dimension to what otherwise would be just another area of exposed female flesh. Slurp. Yodellayeedee!

Now then, what I have to say is that where the country went wrong was not in booting out the last Government, but in booting out the suspender. Slurp. The nation's affairs have gone from Bass to Worthington ever since. Slurp.

It is no accident that during the reign of the suspender man landed on the Moon and sailed single-handed round the world. Only when those hideous tights replaced the suspender did the Moonshots begin to misfire. Remember? 'We have a problem here?' We have a problem here, too. No suspenders.

What this whole scene is about, of course, is erogenous zones. Slurp—yodellayeeeeedeeeee! Ecxuse me! Ever since Eve adjisted her fog leaf, fahsion has dictated the changes on woman's erigxxxx, sorry, erogenous zones from the top of her veiled head to the tip of her peepong toes, taking on the way dwon such diversoins as earlobes, cleavages, sholuder tips, full frontals, full backals anx the stupendous long-running now-you-see-it-now-you-don8t leg x show, of which the all-time hit was the suspinder anx the all-tome loser waz tights (did you ever actuallly see a pair of those things curled up? I mean without legsinthem? Try it simetome, the effect is indescribabable. Slurp. It could put you off wimen all day. Where waz I?

Oh yes, waht we men of the Bring Back the Suspinder Movemetn nogxxxx noticed was that during the reign of tights Britian lost the Wirld Cup and beer taxes went up.

At parties all over the place you8d see women whoes blouses had shrunk or skirts had dropped and there was this area of naked flesh around the bellu-button called the modriff and befreo they knew whre they were they were all sneezing all ove teh places; it wax terrible. Slurpidollogidee!

Now then. What I have ot say is thos. Yuo may have already seen the fahsion exprets predicting that the Suspeneder is coming back under the midis and maxis. Well Great, absitouley grate. As teh old year draws ot a close and hip sprongs etrenal in the human breast for 197; what we must all keep our fingers crissed for is that the new oregonous zone for 197; is going to be the susepender area between the stocking top and thingummies. Slurp—yedellodeee! Anx a Hap;y New yEar ot you all, my frans.